SAM MCAUGHTRY was born in B[...]
World War he was an officer nav[...]
union activist and a well-kno[...]
presenter on radio and TV. *The Sinking of the Kenbane Head*, first
published in 1977 and re-issued here, is his first book and has
been followed by numerous novels and short story collections.
His bestselling memoir, *On the Outside Looking In*, was published
by Blackstaff Press in 2003.

LUDOVIC KENNEDY is an author, television personality and expert
on naval history. His father, Captain Edward C. Kennedy RN, was
lost with most of his crew when his ship, the armed merchant
cruiser *Rawalpindi*, was sunk by enemy action in 1939.

The Sinking of
THE KENBANE HEAD

SAM MCAUGHTRY

Introduction by
LUDOVIC KENNEDY

THE
BLACKSTAFF
PRESS
BELFAST

The final verse of the poem 'The Jervis Bay' by Michael Thwaites is
reproduced by permission of G.P. Putnam, a division of the
Penguin Group Inc.

The Head Line Fleet List is included by permission of the publishers
of *Sea Breezes*, Mannin Media Group Ltd.

The report of the master of the *Kenbane Head*, and its crew list,
appear by permission of Her Majesty's Stationery Office.

The photograph of the *Admiral Scheer* appears by permission
of the Imperial War Museum.

The photographs of Captain Fogarty Fegen (© Vandyk) and
the *Jervis Bay* (© Central Press) appeared in
the *The War Illustrated*, 29 November 1940, p. 567.

Every effort has been made to trace copyright material and the
publishers apologise for any omissions in the above list.

First published in 1977 by Blackstaff Press

This edition published in 2004 by
Blackstaff Press
4c Heron Wharf, Sydenham Business Park
Belfast BT3 9LE
with the assistance of
The Arts Council of Northern Ireland

ARTS
COUNCIL
of Northern Ireland

Typeset by CJWT Solutions, Newton-le-Willows, Merseyside

Printed in Ireland by ColourBooks Limited

A CIP catalogue record for this book is available from the British Library

ISBN 0-85640-763-1

www.blackstaffpress.com

But now thick night was over the sea, and a wind from the
    west blew keen,
And the hopeless waters tossed their heads where the *Jervis Bay*
    had been,
And the raider was lost in the rain and the night, and low
    clouds hid the seas,
But high above sea and storm and cloud appeared the galaxies,
And the big stars called the little stars that had not dared to
    peep,
And all the stars of heaven came out across the heaving deep,
And they shone bright over the good shepherd of the sheep.

from 'The Jervis Bay'
MICHAEL THWAITES

CONTENTS

PREFACE

The Sinking of the Kenbane Head, first published in 1977, is about a Second World War naval action, the death of a much loved brother, and my growing up in the 1920s and 30s — in sore poverty, one of a family of ten — in a strongly loyalist area of North Belfast. Apart from the details of the sinking of a little cargo ship by a powerful enemy, and the loss of twenty-three of her crew in the bitter cold of the North Atlantic in 1940, the social content of the story — and the notion of Protestant poverty — attracted enough attention throughout this island for the first edition to sell out quickly and for me to travel and make friends in all of the thirty-two counties of Ireland.

The book is a memorial to my brother and my mother, herself the product of a mixed marriage, who taught me tolerance and understanding. She brought us up on her own, because my father was mostly at sea; she lost four children from disease; but in our family laughter outvoted crying by a landslide.

Many of those whose help with the book is

acknowledged – the survivors of the disaster, and their loved ones back home – have passed on. We became firm friends in the writing of the work, and they are greatly missed. New readers will not just learn of hard times in old times: they will, I hope, enjoy in these pages the humour and goodwill that helped us to rise above the hardship of our lives. These are qualities still to be seen today, and are just as necessary, for poverty and intolerance, like rust, never sleep.

SAM McAUGHTRY
COMBER, COUNTY DOWN
2004

FOREWORD

The war ended all of thirty years ago and more, and yet for those of us who took part in it, it still remains one of the most vivid periods of our lives. Especially was this true of the war at sea under both Red and White Ensigns; for living in a ship, year in year out, enduring the grey monotony of watches, seeing nothing but the sea, sharing the close comradeship of one's fellows, in good times and bad, was an experience like no other.

There have been many books about personal wartime experiences, but this one is different. It tells of the author's childhood in a 'two-up two-down' in North Belfast, of the home from which the father and later his adored brother set out and returned to after long spells at sea. He wanted to join them of course, but his mother was against it, and there was no money for an apprenticeship. I like the way in which Mr McAughtry follows one chapter on life at home with another on the course of the war in the Atlantic: it is only at the end, when brother Mart is in the convoy attacked by the *Admiral Scheer*, that the two worlds meet.

It is not easy to write again of the stories of such warships as the *Scheer* and the *Hipper*, the *Rawalpindi* and the *Jervis Bay*. Yet Mr McAughtry does so with freshness and commendable historical accuracy. And in his descriptions of school and family life in pre-war Belfast he proves himself a natural storyteller.

I hope others will enjoy his book as much as I have done.

LUDOVIC KENNEDY
1977

AUTHOR'S NOTE

The following survived the sinking of the *Kenbane Head* and told me their stories: Jimmy Dickey, Chief Steward; Bill McBride, Able Seaman; Gerry Crangle and Norman Walsh, both apprentices in 1940 and now masters.

Mrs Pamela McCready let me have copies of letters written by her late husband, Hugh, passenger on the *Kenbane Head*; Mrs Grace Coates spoke to me about her brother Donald McKay, AB, lost in the action; Mrs Belshaw gave me material concerning her husband, the *Kenbane Head*'s carpenter, also lost; Mrs Turner let me have her recollections of her brother, Robert Moore, who died in the action. Mary Lonergan's sweetheart, Jim Swain, fireman, survived the ordeal but was lost two years later, and Mary was kind enough to tell me about it.

For further important background material I am indebted to: Jim McIntosh, second radio officer, SS *Mopan*; Fred Heatley, ex–Head Line donkeyman; Billy Dickey, once chief steward in the Line; Captain E.W. Black OBE, last commodore of the Head Line; Captain H.C. Thompson, and Mr J.F. Milner, son of Captain Milner, master of the *Kenbane Head*.

Tragically, Seamus O'Hara, one-time donkeyman, died soon after giving me valuable background material. To his widow Bessie, to those others named above, and to the many helpful people who assisted me in researching this book, I offer my deepest gratitude.

SAM McAUGHTRY
BELFAST, 1977

1
HAPPY DAYS

My father was a small man, neat and trim. Very cool and collected. His eyes were sea-blue and his fine brown hair was brushed to the side. His nose was on the big side. It was criss-crossed with bluey purple veins.

Blue noses were fairly common among my father's shipmates. I used to think this was odd. It certainly wasn't caused by the elements, for Dad and most of his shore-going companions worked in the engine room and when he wasn't there he was in the fo'c's'le. It might have been drink that did it.

When you consider the thousands of back-breaking hours that seamen like my father spent shovelling coal in bunkers and stokeholds, beginning in nineteenth-century iron steamers, you would expect them to be built like gorillas, wouldn't you? In fact my dad stripped to about nine stone, and his muscles were more like silk than steel.

Nearly all the ships' firemen and trimmers I met were like that as well. Small to medium.

Considering the living accommodation they were provided with, maybe it's just as well they weren't big men.

Everybody called him Mark but his real name was Marriott, a name used in our family for many generations.

A seafaring Marriott McAughtry is buried in St Nicholas' Church, Carrickfergus, under a headstone that is 150 years old.

Born in 1882, my dad first went to sea in 1897. He married my mother Lizzie in 1909 and they started their family with Jack in 1911. Nine more children were to come.

Marriott was next, born in 1913. We called him Mart.

Mart was a smashing fellow to have for a brother. I am writing this book so that I can pay tribute to him.

Tommy was next, then Chattie, or Charlotte. A boy, Sam, was born next but he died after only a few days. I came along in 1921. I wasn't a terrible lot stronger than the child before me who had died. They nearly put the jinx on me altogether by giving me his name – Sam – but one way and another I managed to hang on long enough to get a grip in amongst the rest of the family.

With all these kids coming along our house in Cosgrave Street in North Belfast was getting a bit crowded. It was only a two-up two-down. Four more kids came after me, starting with Jim, born in 1923. Betty made her appearance after that, to be followed by Harry and Molly.

Betty, Harry and Molly all died within a few years. None of them lived beyond the age of four.

Molly died of a baby's complaint, at only a few months old. Harry, well, Harry's death was a bad business. My mother had put Jim and myself in one bed and Betty and Harry in another in the same room at about seven o'clock one evening. Then she went out to the backyard to do her washing and mangling.

Harry was eleven months old and already he was able to

walk a few steps. He was lying crowing to himself contentedly enough, when Mother left him. She washed for about twenty minutes and then took a look upstairs to see how things were. Well, here's how things were: Harry was hanging by his nightdress from the end of the bed. He had tried to walk a few steps across the bed and his nightdress had caught on the brass knob at the foot of the bed. He was stone dead when Mother found him.

Next thing we knew Betty died. Of whooping cough. She was four years old. I was about seven at the time and I can remember the fire being lit in the bedroom – a sure sign of sickness. The women of the family were tiptoeing about the house and the night before she died there was talk of The Crisis.

I remember thinking The Crisis was a man. In a white robe, like Christ. This was probably because Mother kept telling people in a whisper: 'The Crisis is coming tonight.'

It didn't half come. When it left Betty went with it. She was a wee mischievous imp, with a donkey fringe and dancing eyes. It just happened that she had had a studio picture taken shortly before her illness. The print was enlarged and framed and it hung up in our house for years.

My father loved Betty very dearly. When she died he wore a black tie and he never wore any other sort of tie for the rest of his life and that was twenty-three years more. He also hung a smaller framed picture of her in his tiny cabin on the *Dunaff Head*.

The frame would still be there, I suppose, lying at the bottom of the North Atlantic near Iceland, but the photo itself will have gone long ago.

We had a good long run after that before anybody else

died. Still, four kids lost out of ten was rough sledding for any woman, and her man away at sea too.

I'm telling you, my mother knew all about the hard times back in the Hungry Twenties, all right. It's no wonder she was wild religious.

My father did most of his voyaging in ships of the Head Line fleet, owned by the Ulster Steamship Company – G. Heyn & Sons.

This company was first registered in Belfast in 1877, and very soon afterwards a shipping merchant with an unfulfilled ambition took over the firm, and its solitary ship, the iron steamer *Bickley*. He was Gustavus Heyn, from Danzig. With his sons James and Fritz he rapidly began to build up a fleet.

It was Gustavus Heyn who adopted the custom of naming his ships after Irish headlands, and before many years had passed the Head Line ships and their distinctive Red Hand of Ulster funnel markings were familiar sights in the ports of the Baltic and the Eastern seaboard of America.

The history of the Head Line fleet up to 1940 is set out in the next chapter. Its story is the story of the achievements of my father and many tough seamen like him. It was men like these who conferred on the Heyn family, from the outset, a proud and enduring reputation as reliable cargo carriers.

I have in my possession my father's discharge books covering the period February 1904 to February 1941. The discharge book that followed those must have been lost with my father's other effects when the *Dunaff Head* was torpedoed in March 1941. He got off the ship with only the clothes he was wearing.

In any case he must have been issued with a further one when he went back to sea in the *Empire Outpost* after getting back to fitness again (don't forget he was fifty-nine when the *Dunaff Head* went down), but this one, too, is missing. It showed his last ten years' voyaging in what he reckoned were the most comfortable ships he ever sailed in – the fleet belonging to Headlam and Sons of Whitby.

It might be of interest to see the contents of his discharge books summarised. Actually the real title of the book is the Continuous Certificate of Discharge. Inside is shown, for each voyage, the name and official number of the ship and its registered tonnage, the date and place of the seaman's engagement, the seaman's rating, the date and place of discharge, a short description of the voyage, the master's signature, and the report of the seaman's character and ability during the voyage.

My father's oldest discharge book was, in fact, a replacement for an earlier one lost. Heaven knows how it was lost, for I gather he was a bit of a lad when he was single. In fact, he had been seafaring for seven years already, when the first discharge book was issued to him.

From February 1904 until November 1909 he sailed in the *Torr Head*, completing eighteen voyages in that time, to Canada, the USA, South America, Australia and the Baltic. He was a trimmer in the *Torr Head* for the first nine voyages, a fireman for two trips after that, a greaser for one trip and a storekeeper for six voyages.

He had one trip in the *Dunmore Head* on the Baltic run as a fireman and trimmer at the end of 1909 and two in the

Glenarm Head as a greaser between February and October 1910, both voyages being to South America. Then he did twenty-four consecutive trips in the *Ramore Head*, starting as fireman and trimmer for the first two, sailing as storekeeper for thirteen voyages and donkeyman – senior rating – for the last nine. Most of these trips were to the eastern Canadian and USA ports.

This took him up to August 1915, when the First World War was exactly a year old. He then signed on the White Star liner *Olympic*, a troop ship, as a greaser. He went from her to the *San Rito* and sailed to Port Said in this little ship of less than two thousand tons. One trip as storekeeper in the *City of Perth* in early 1917, then he went back to the Head Line, signing on the *Melmore Head* as a fireman and trimmer.

On 4 July 1920 my father began an association with the *Dunaff Head* as storekeeper and then donkeyman that was to last, with the exception of a short break, right up until she was torpedoed in 1941. The break came between November 1923 and October 1924, when he did two trips in the *Ramore Head* to the Baltic, one trip to New Zealand in the *Port Wellington* and another to Canada in the *Kenbane Head*, signing on as fireman for all four voyages.

In all, my father signed on the *Dunaff Head* no less than ninety-two times, including the trip when she was torpedoed. A few of the trips were to the Far East, South America and Australia, but the vast majority of his voyages were to North America, where the Head Line's regular income lay.

This association was broken only because there was hardly any Head Line fleet left when the *Dunaff* went down. My father signed on with another company for the last ten years of his life.

For some reason, the Head Line forgot to thank him for his contribution, which, as a matter of interest, amounted to 140 recorded voyages in Head Line ships between 1904 and 1941, plus a conservative estimate of a further 20 in the 7 unrecorded years before 1904.

That's 160 trips. Mostly across the North Atlantic. There are seamen who did more for the Head Line, but I don't think the company wrote thank you letters to them either.

Talking about discharge books, our Jim and I, who were considered to be far too young for such things, once had a fascinating time going through the record of Dad's voyages in order to pinpoint the dates on which each of our keels were laid, so to speak.

On 6 June 1910 the old man paid off from the *Glenarm Head* at North Shields, on which he had sailed for the previous four months on a voyage to South America and back.

Me and our Jim worked it out, when I was about nine and he was seven. Yes, we said. That's about right. Jack was born in March 1911. The kids in the street must be right about that stuff.

Two years later Dad paid off the *Ramore Head* after a two-month trip to Canada. OK, let's see, said the two young researchers. Yes. Mmmmm. Mart was born in March 1913, was he not?

Marvellous. Here's yours Sam. Oh? Where, exactly? There. Look. On 17 June 1920, at the port of Belfast,

Marriott McAughtry, fireman and trimmer, walked down the gangway of the SS *Melmore Head*, lately arrived from Montreal. He was glad to be home.

My date of birth is 24 March 1921, if anybody wants to know.

My father's father was a master mariner. That's how it was always referred to in our house: master mariner. Never sea captain. The old man's side of the family were all very proud of this. Especially his mother, Mary, my Gramma.

'Your grandfather John McAughtry was a master mariner,' she used to say to me when I visited her in her little house in Shandon Street by the New Lodge Road.

For the life of me I could never understand why Gramma kept bringing this up. We hadn't two halfpennies to scratch ourselves with, so Captain John couldn't have been master of a very big ship.

Gramma was very old indeed, to my young mind. She commanded immense respect from our breed, seed and generation, not only because she had probably the highest IQ in the connection. Gramma, even in her eighties, was nimble of mind and deft in debate. She had a firmer grasp of politics and economics than any man of her acquaintance. Very likely she picked up the reading habit when she went to sea the odd time with my grandfather.

Incidentally, Captain John died at thirty-nine, drowned in Liverpool dock. We never bothered looking into the circumstances. Dad was sent to identify his body in 1897. He arranged for it to be sent home and then he took off at the age of fifteen, working down below, in some tramp or other. He didn't come home to Belfast for two years. And bingo went the chance of the Macs producing another master mariner. Gramma lost a lot of her fancy for Dad after that.

She was small and she wore long, black clothes. Her grey hair was pulled back in a bun. She wore rimless glasses with wool wrapped around the connecting piece so that it wouldn't cut into her nose.

The bottoms of her eyes were red crescents where the membrane had fallen downwards and the flesh underneath her chin had dropped so that it wobbled when she turned her head.

She was a tough old bird was Gramma. During the blitz on Belfast, when she was eighty-three, a 250-pounder dropped on to Shandon Street, bringing the house down around her. The neighbours dug her out of the parlour where she had been sleeping. Dusty and in a foul temper she was brought the few hundred yards to our house in Hillman Street.

'Here you are, Gramma,' my mother said, handing her a cup of tea.

'Have you anything else?' she asked, delicately. We knew what she meant.

'Try this,' said Mother, handing her a glass of brandy. She sniffed at it suspiciously, her face grimy and her hair and clothes covered in cement dust.

'Thanks, Lizzie,' she said. 'I hope you haven't watered it. It destroys it, you know,' and then she sank it in one, and that was the blitz dealt with.

It was a custom in our family that the job of washing and laying out the dead fell to Gramma. It was she who laid out

Betty and Harry and Molly and the other Sam in our family. I happened to pass the bedroom door after Betty died and saw the naked little body lying on top of the bed whilst Gramma was holding her burial clothes up, examining them. I'll always remember that. Wee Betty looked so defenceless or something.

Gramma lived long enough to wash and lay out my own mother in 1946. She died herself not long after, and we worded her death notice with care: 'Mary McAughtry, widow of John McAughtry, Master Mariner ...'

Whenever his ship tied up my father followed a strict ritual. As soon as he had finished wiping down the engines he came up on deck from the engine room and collected a bucket of hot water from the galley. He carried this up on to the fo'c's'le head, stepping over the two-foot high breakwater that ran slantwise across the deck. Then he descended into the port side of the fo'c's'le, where the engine room crew had their quarters. There he undressed and scrubbed himself pink-clean.

Dressed in his shore-going navy blue suit, white shirt and black tie, he hoisted his long, seaman's bag on to his shoulder and went down the gangway, out into Whitla Street, and into Phil Maguire's pub nearby. With him usually were his pals the bo'sun and lamptrimmer. In Phil Maguire's they bevied for a couple of hours.

Around about this time, his family were in a fine state of excitement, back in Cosgrave Street. This street was built on a steep hill that looked straight down on the docks, where the ocean-going ships tied up. Often it was possible to see from our street Dad's ship move slowly into view as she berthed. Her outline was unmistakable – all the Head Line ships carried the emblem of the Ulster Steamship Company, the Red Hand of Ulster on a white shield. The funnel and hull were painted black, and the upper works were white and yellow.

The shipping news in the *Belfast Telegraph* would have alerted us the day before the ship was due in any case, but all the way across the last leg of her journey I would have been following her course. Pinned up in the reading room of the Belfast Public Library was a copy of Lloyd's *Shipping Gazette*, and the noon position of Dad's ship was there. It was only a matter, for a school kid like me, of standing on tiptoe and looking for it.

'*Dunaff Head*, noon 25 January. Bar 40, vis. 15, NW Force 3, bound Belfast', it would say, giving the ship's position. I would sit on the hot pipes in the reading room, get my atlas out of my schoolbag, and check the noon position myself.

As the time drew near for the old man to arrive home, Mother was a sight to see. She, too, was scrubbed pink, with a touch of powder added. Her soft, dark hair was tied back in a bun. A brand new pinny was produced for each homecoming. She kept pulling and smoothing at this.

Mother was small, like Dad, and sonsy. At the least excitement a round spot would glow on each of her cheeks. They were there in her cheeks all right, in the run-up to Dad's homecoming. She would shush us kids when anticipation made us noisy, but we could see she was pretty thrilled at this time.

My goodness, they were in love, those two. In all my life I have never seen a married couple who were so much in love. There she was having given him ten kids, waiting at the door of our cramped little house, looking eagerly down the cobbled street for the taxi that would bring her man home to her from the sea.

When he arrived they would hug just inside the tiny kitchen, two small people, all dressed up for each other, in an ocean of love, with me and the other kids looking on and thinking the whole thing was absolutely smashing.

They didn't wait around too long downstairs at this stage. First Mother rushed to make him a cup of milky tea, while Dad produced silver for each of us out of his waistcoat pocket. Then they both went upstairs for the best part of a couple of hours.

And downstairs we young ones were steeped in contentment. Daddy was home from the sea. The house was full of a lovely smell of whiskey and Woodbines, and we had silver in our pockets.

Nobody in the world could have been happier than we were when the *Dunaff Head* came home.

2

BACKGROUND

THE HEAD LINE FLEET LIST
1877–1940

NAME	DATE BUILT	GROSS TONS	REMARKS
Bickley	1877	631	Stranded near Tobermore, 6 October 1884
Fair Head	1879	1,175	Sold 1934, renamed *City of Waterford*
White Head	1880	1,192	Torpedoed and sunk 40 miles NNE Suda Bay, 15 October 1917
Black Head	1881	1,191	Stranded and became total loss on Bornholm, 25 January 1912
Teelin Head	1883	1,781	Torpedoed and sunk 12 miles SSW Owers Light Vessel, 21 January 1918
Bengore Head	1884	2,490	Sunk by submarine, NW Fastnet, 20 June 1917
Horn Head	1884	2,386	Missing in N. Atlantic, 1894
Inishowen Head	1886	3,050	Torpedoed and sunk off Skokhom Island, 14 February 1917
Dunmore Head	1889	2,293	Torpedoed and sunk NW of Tory Island, April 1917
Ramore Head	1891	4,444	Sold 1924 to German breakers
Bray Head	1894	3,150	Sunk by submarine W of Fastnet, 20 March 1917

Torr Head	1894	5,911	Sunk by submarine SW of Ireland, April 1917
Glen Head	1883 acquired 1895	1,600	Ex–*Nant Gwynant*. Wrecked on Bornholm, 9 December 1934
Malin Head	1892 acquired 1896	3,467	Ex–*A.J. Balfour*. Stranded Pentland Firth, 21 October 1910
Glenarm Head	1897	3,908	Sunk by submarine off Brighton, January 1918
Rathlin Head	1899	6,754	Broken up at Rosyth, 1929
Carrigan Head	1901	4,201	Broken up at Rosyth, June 1934
Howth Head	1906	4,440	Sunk by submarine N. Atlantic, 22 April 1917
Black Head	1912	1,898	Torpedoed and sunk 52 miles ESE of Outer Skerries, Shetlands, 21 June 1917
Garron Head	1913	1,933	Mined 40 miles NE of Bayonne, 16 November 1917
Orlock Head	1913	1,945	Captured and sunk by gunfire by U-34, 65 miles SE of Barcelona, 12 April 1916
Fanad Head	1917	5,200	Sunk by submarine S of Rockall, 14 September 1939
Lord Antrim	1902 acquired 1917	4,665	Sold and broken up 1934
Lord Downshire	1900 acquired 1917	5,223	Sold and broken up 1929
Dunaff Head	1918	5,877	Sunk by submarine S of Iceland, 7 March 1941
Melmore Head	1918	5,319	Sunk by submarine N of Azores, 28 December 1942
Ballygally Head	1919	5,155	Sold 1924, renamed *Kepwickhall*

Kenbane Head	1919	5,155	Sunk by *Admiral Scheer*, SE of Greenland, 5 November 1940
Wicklow Head	1879 acquired 1919	1,453	Ex–*City of Munich*, ex-*Hungarian*. Sold 1933 and renamed *City of Ghent*
Lord Londonderry	1902 acquired 1920	5,796	Ex-*Schonfels*. Broken up December 1934
Orlock Head	1921	1,563	Sunk by aircraft off Strathie Pt, 28 July 1940
Dunmore Head	1922	2,503	Sold while fitting out to Hogarths, renamed *Baron Vernon*
Bengore Head	1922	2,609	Torpedoed and sunk by submarine in Denmark Strait, 9 May 1941
Torr Head	1923	5,221	Sold to Chilean owners September 1933 and renamed *Angol*
Dunmore Head	1898 acquired 1924	1,682	Ex-*Reval*. Taken over by Royal Navy as ammunition hulk, 1939
Teelin Head	1897	903	Ex-*Audierne*, ex-*Doonass*, ex-*Whimbrel*. Sold 1934, renamed *City of Bremen*
Fair Head	1906	1,719	Ex-*Zealand*. Bombed at Belfast, 5 May 1941
Glen Head	1909	2,011	Ex-*Penthames*, ex–*Comtesse de Flandre*, ex-*Neva*. Bombed SW of Cape St Vincent, 6 June 1941
Torr Head	1937	5,021	Survived World War II

3
UNCLE THOMAS
1927

A wisp of paper caught in a wind eddy soared to roof height and, watching from Cosgrave Street below, I took flight with it. Up, up and over the moss-tinted slate acres to the clear sky beyond, in the favourite flight-dream that bubbled its way more often than any other to the top of my mind, rising through the tumble of wonderings and fancies that were there.

The laugh of the childless woman at the door brought me back, startled.

'You were miles away. Away up in the sky. Weren't you?'

Arms folded, she looked at me with a fond intensity. I turned away and ran off up the narrow street, past Newington Church. Here the bumpy cobblestones changed to sound-absorbent tarmac so that the horses' iron shoes and the heavy cartwheels would not shut out the voice of God from the Presbyterian women, with their iron stays, who worshipped in the church.

I turned the corner to the left, still running and skipping, then veered hard right into Collyer Street, stopping at number seventy-one. By a faint shade the people in this street seemed poorer than those in my own. The houses seemed even more tightly pressed together. They were not brightened up by the teams of out-of-work shipyard tradesmen who passed by regularly, offering to paint window frames and sill for sixpence.

The people who lived in Collyer Street could not even afford the single pennies that bought music from the mandolin and banjo players with blacking on their faces – pattern-makers and riveters in disguise.

In this street Uncle Thomas was the top earner, with an income of fifteen shillings to a pound a day from the docks. With only himself to keep he was the richest man in the street.

I pushed the front door open. The house smelt empty. No smell of broth simmering, or of the rock-hard ling fish undergoing its hours of boiling and softening. No underlay of soapsuds; the house lacked the smell of a family.

The floor had no lino, just red tiles that were swept but not washed. A scrubbed, bare table sat by the window. The only other piece of furniture was an ancient oak sideboard by the wall opposite the window.

The house was still. Its quietness excited me; breaking the rules was marvellously exciting. I tiptoed into the scullery. There, by the jawbox, were the usual black bottles. Their smell was Uncle Thomas's when he came home in the evenings in his dungarees and the jacket with the torn left shoulder. The pockets of his jacket were filled with Indian corn and Uncle Thomas would stand at the front door, his arm around me, and feed the pigeons that clustered around the door. The street-hokers fought among the cobblestones for the corn, their fat throats wobbling with greed.

And often Uncle Thomas would be joined at his front

door by the children of the street, and I would feel uneasy and a little ashamed as he encouraged them to sing, for pennies, the hymns that they had learned in the mission in Tiger's Bay, at the top of Collyer Street.

A very respectable family who lived opposite Uncle Thomas were members of the Salvation Army, and he would line the children up opposite this house and get them to sing about two shillings worth of hymns, just to aggravate the Salvationists. 'General Booth!' Uncle Thomas would shout at the quiet, inoffensive house. 'General Booth! The Army's on parade!' That's the time I used to be ashamed.

He was small, and dark like my mother and Uncles Hugh, Sammy and James, and Aunts Berry and Lena, for he was a member of their family. His upper lip had once been split, and this pulled his mouth down to one side. There was a deep scar at the side of his right eye. The palms of his hands were iron-hard. He was the black sheep of the family, and he was afraid of nothing and no one. I liked him very much and was also a little afraid of him. Sometimes he called into our house drunk, and bantered Mother the way he bantered the Salvationists. She didn't take it lying down, but nevertheless it was a bit worrying for me when it happened.

The jacket that Uncle Thomas wore was ripped and torn at the shoulder, right to the canvas lining. On this shoulder he had carried thousands of lengths of timber and hundredweight sacks of grain, loading and unloading the deep-sea boats. When his work was done for the day he and the rest of the squad would gather in one of the dockside pubs and there the stevedores paid them their daily wage in silver. Unless he was having one of his infrequent spells off the beer Uncle Thomas stayed after his day's work, drinking in the pub, until hunger and fatigue drove him home.

I liked it when the front door was shut and Uncle Thomas set me up to the bare table to join him at his evening meal. 'Eat that meat up now,' he would urge. 'It's good for you. Get plenty of that fat down you – if you ate more fat you wouldn't be so delicate,' and as he finished he would look critically at my thin arms and knobbly knees.

I would show him how I could write, producing a specimen kept specially for him. 'You're going to be a scholar,' Uncle Thomas would say, waving his fork, smiling. The grease from the hot broth and meat chunks traversed the porter tracks at the side of his mouth.

In those days I thought that being a scholar had something to do with being delicate.

Tiptoeing in the empty house was different though, and better. From the centre of the kitchen I looked around. On the wall hung an old oil painting of a coastal schooner. The sea's blue had turned to black and the gilt of the frame was lost to the dust of many years.

On the mantelpiece were two brass candlesticks, dull and neglected. They were the only ornaments in the tiny room. Above and between them hung an oval, faded picture of a soft-eyed woman. She wore a white lace blouse, her dark hair was piled high on her head, and her smile was a faint, shy smile worn by everyone I knew, when formality entered their lives.

This was Uncle Thomas's mother. She was my mother's mother. As usual, when I peered at it, the kindly eyes knew me. Looking up at the picture I wondered, as always, how she had actually gone up to heaven. Did she rise one day on the wind and fly through the clouds up towards the stars?

It was getting late. Mother would soon be making the evening meal for us. There was just time to do what I wanted. I knelt before the oak sideboard and, opening the door, brought out an old, brown lacquered box. I lifted the lid. At the bottom of the box was a creased original of the picture on the wall. Lying in a confused pile on top of the photograph was a set of rosary beads.

I held the beads out. There were certainly plenty of them, I thought. Putting them around my neck, I studied myself, looking down. Then I took them off.

I stood up and moved the usual chair to its usual place before the fireplace. Climbing up on the chair I stood in front of the picture so that I looked into the eyes that were so like my own. I held the beads out between my two forefingers, level with the slender neck in the picture. They hung perfectly, meeting in a vee within the frame, the foot of the pendant cross just above the bottom edge.

Tilting my head back, I studied the effect critically. With thin, serious face and pursed lips I looked at the picture of the soft-eyed woman and the beads that I had given her. As always I looked finally directly into her eyes and nodded slightly. Then I got quickly down from the chair, replaced the beads in the box on top of the photograph, and put the box back in the sideboard out of sight.

Pulling Uncle Thomas's front door carefully after me I ran off down Collyer Street, along Robina Street, and into Cosgrave Street. The lamps were casting their yellow light on the cobbled road and footpath, and glittering new frost was forming. Seeing the dancing diamonds at my feet the flight-dream came back. Suddenly I was running across the night sky high, high above the narrow streets.

As I ran I wondered what made the diamonds dance, and I wondered if my mother's mother liked her beads, and, as I drew near to our house I was wondering whether she could see me from heaven, running across the sky and over the stars.

When I was a kid I was sickly and used to hang around the house a lot. This used frequently to get on the nerves of the older ones in the family. It was hardly surprising when you consider that seven of us had to coexist in a room measuring three yards by three that had to serve as dining room, sitting room, playroom and lounge. Many a time between the ages of six and nine I was told by a couple of older brothers to clear off outside, for dear sake, and stop forever hanging around the house like some wee girl or something. Many a time there was a push or a cuff along with it too, in the way of young people. But never, never, never was my brother Marriott one of those who chivvied me.

Mart was my protector; my Alpha and Omega. He was for me the sun, the moon and the stars. Starting as my sure shield and watchdog he became my great friend, and then my idol.

When I was eight, Mart was sixteen and unemployed. He was five foot eight, with a physique that was almost perfect – powerful shoulders, deep chest, narrow hips and slim legs.

He had the slightly flat-footed walk of the natural ball-player. His cheek bones were high and pronounced, and his skin was tight to his face and forehead. Because he was so good at football the headmaster of our school, Mr Topping, paid Mart half a crown a week to coach the school team. In addition to this a man called Moore who lived at the foot of Cave Hill paid him five shillings a week to exercise his greyhound on the slopes of the hill.

When I was allowed to go with Mart to watch the school team play, or to roam the foot of Black Mountain with the greyhound, it was a marvellous treat. He didn't talk a lot, just listened to my flow of chatter intently, as though I was grown-up, instead of a rundown glandular kid whose stories were half-imagined anyway.

He was some man, my brother Mart. I have never met anybody who was as good as he was. That's why I'm writing this book about him. It makes me feel as if I'm in very close touch with him.

4
BACKGROUND
DOWN BELOW

In the 1920s and 1930s a first-tripper going down below in a deep-water Head Line ship was in for a rough time of it. Nothing that he might have done ashore in the way of work could possibly condition him for the abrupt change that seafaring was to bring to his way of life.

In 1927 one starry-eyed young fellow of twenty was told by his father, storekeeper in the Head Line, that there was a berth for him on a ship as a trimmer. The lad's knowledge of seafaring was confined to his dad's arrival home every few months, dressed neatly, and with cash enough in his pockets to tip the kids handsomely, buy his mother a present, and stand the drinks for two or three nights at the pub round the corner. An aura of adventure was added by the American-style cold weather clothes that his father sometimes wore, and by the foreign stamps that his letters bore.

Going to sea! Philadelphia, Montreal, Quebec, Three Rivers! What tales this young man was going to tell his mates from the factories and the building sites, when he came home!

His mother, thoughtful and quiet, bought his gear: heavy

boots, stout overalls and flannel shirts, two sets of underclothing, half a dozen pairs of woollen socks. She reminded him to take his muffler for going ashore in Canada and he shivered in delightful anticipation.

'I'd rather he didn't have to go to that rough oul' work,' she said to his father. 'Sure I don't want it either, love,' he said, 'but there's nothing else.'

The company had a rule about joining the ship in those days. You could come aboard any time you liked on the day she sailed, but you weren't on the strength until five past midnight and the ship sailed as soon as possible afterwards. That way the company saved money. Another way all companies saved money was by paying low wages. In the 1920s and 1930s a fireman and trimmer earned £9.10 a month, a greaser got £1.00 more, a storekeeper £1.10 more and a donkeyman £2.10 a month more than a fireman.

But what did our young lad care about pay? He was walking down alongside the ship with his dad, each carrying the long seaman's bag over one shoulder, and with their mattresses under the other arm. Known as the 'donkey's breakfast', the Head Line sailors were required to provide their own straw mattresses. These were bought at half a crown a time from a ship's chandler in Princes Dock Street.

The lad's father had referred only once to the experience that lay ahead. That had been in the taxi a few minutes earlier after his mother had kissed her son a tearful goodbye, and his younger brother had awkwardly shaken his hand for the first time in his life.

'Look,' said his dad, 'the first trip is always rough. The

firemen can't help you very much, for they'll be busy enough. Get stuck in. Don't think about anything and you won't get sick. Just keep working, and you'll be OK.'

As he went up the gangway behind his father the young chap, for the first time, began to realise that he was now a working seaman – it was no pleasure cruise that lay ahead.

The gangway led amidships. Along forrard they went, down one ladder and up another one – awkward this, for the first-tripper carrying his gear – stepping over the breakwater on the fo'c's'le head, the older man led the way to the entrance to the crew's quarters, two doors protected by a curved scuttle; port for the engine room crew and starboard for the sailors. Down the port steps they went, to find themselves in a gloomily-lit mess room. A number of men were sitting around the mess table, still in shore-going clothes. Some of them seemed to have had a few drinks, but none to any marked degree.

The father was greeted good-humouredly and the son was introduced around. He was struck particularly by the strong bond of comradeship that was evident among them.

The young fellow found that he had to bunk up with eight others right up in the bows, the steel plates of the ship's side only inches from him when he lay down. Six firemen and three trimmers were accommodated here in pairs of bunks fixed tight to the bows, where the ship rose and fell and lurched and battered her way through the waves.

Just before midnight the second engineer slid expertly down the steps into the fo'c's'le and began to set the watches, calling out the names of the crew from a list in his hand. There was another first-tripper. 'Two trimmers out of three are first-trippers, boys,' the second engineer said with a wink. 'She's gonna go slow on this leg!'

Our chap was on the twelve to four watch. His dad was on the eight to twelve. One of the older firemen whispered in his ear, 'The eight to twelve's the best. You can sleep when the ship's quiet.' Before many days were over the young newcomer was to know only too well what he meant, especially when, after tumbling exhausted into his bunk at half past four in the morning, he was awakened at half past eight by a sailor chipping the deck over his head.

The donkeyman took him up on deck, along amidships, though the fiddley and into the bunkers. He explained the routine. There were two firemen to a watch; one fireman tended five fires, the other looked after four, and one trimmer kept three chutes filled with coal for the firemen. The job was straightforward. Very little explanation was necessary. You are alone in this great gloomy cavern with a coal floor. Here is the shovel – there are the chutes. Keep them filled. When you had cleared the space around the chutes, here is a barrow, fill it, wheel the coal to the chutes and tip it into them.

When the donkeyman had gone and he was alone, in his brand new dungarees and brand new boots, about to start making up the space in the chute which the firemen were already beginning to create, he was startled by a loud voice from up above, calling his name.

'I'm Captain Finlay,' the owner of the voice shouted. 'Yes, Captain,' the first-tripper said nervously (God – the Captain!).

'I've just noticed that you've signed on as a fireman and trimmer,' shouted the captain. 'Well, you'll be doing just trimming this trip – no firing. That means you'll get ten shillings a month less. All right?'

'Right y'are, Captain,' the young man said and he heard the captain grunt as he went back on deck again.

For the first hour or so it wasn't too bad. He had plenty of wind, it seemed. The coal hadn't far to go. Without having the time to pay much attention to it he realised that the ship was moving out of Belfast, bound for Greenock, the coaling port, and then to St John's New Brunswick. As his back, shoulders, arms and legs began to protest at the pace of the shovelling he had to do, it occurred to the young man for a fleeting moment that this was not the way he had imagined he would sail out of Belfast port. Somehow in the picture he had carried in his mind he had seen himself leaning out from one of the bridge wings, smiling sardonically at the dockside watchers, turning to go below to write his first letter home …

Now, what had been a gentle rolling movement developed into a decided pitch. It upset his calculations with the barrow. Worse than that, it caused him sometimes to tip the barrow over when it was nowhere near the chute. The blood was beginning to pound in his head with the physical effort of trimming the coal and supplying the firemen. It seemed that he had been wrong in two matters – firstly, the watch must be eight hours long and not four, he must already have been six hours in this goddam hole; and secondly, there must be about nine bloody firemen down there, all working like frigpots. After what seemed like seven hours' labour he heard one of the firemen hail him.

'Hey. What about a drop of tea?'

He knew about this duty. Hanging up in the bunker was a 'growler' – a seven-pound jam tin with a wire strung across the top for a handle. He picked this up and went up top through the fiddley to the galley, where the watch on deck would keep the fire going until the cook came on watch in the morning. A pot was boiling on the plate and he poured the scalding water on top of the tea and took it down to the sweating firemen in the stokehold. They punched him gently in friendship: 'You're doing OK,' they told him. 'Doing great.' But he learned with sick dismay that he was only half way through his watch; he hadn't even time to join them for a mug of tea.

Later, in the fo'c's'le, when the first watch had somehow or other come to an end, he thought that he could sleep for a week. But, when the first-tripper found himself in his bunk, facing steel plates that dripped with condensation, and lying on a strange prickly straw mattress, sleep came only fitfully. Time and time again he awoke, at first terrified by the unexpected, violent movement at the ship's bows, or angry and frustrated because of the incessant pounding vibration of the ship's engines, and the crashing impact transmitted through the hull as the steamer bulldozed her way through the Irish Sea.

He lowered himself stiffly over the side of his bunk at eight in the morning unable to sleep, resigned to sitting around in a sleepy stupor until he next turned-to at noon. The arrival of the other first-tripper in the fo'c's'le, however, made him feel that things could have been a whole lot worse. The other chap looked like death. He was in the grip of chronic seasickness, and when he collapsed weakly at the mess table and made to rest his head in his hands, the palms were seen to be torn and bleeding. Our young chap could only stare in awe at the condition of his shipmate.

'There's only one thing for seasickness,' one of the off-watch firemen told the rocking victim, 'eat away there and don't worry about it.'

After trying vainly to help, our young fellow stuck his cap on his head, and went up on deck, where he lay over the fo'c's'le rail, staring at the Scottish coast just becoming visible ahead.

At last, and in a totally unexpected way, he felt like a seaman ...

And he worked his way on the twelve to four, to Greenock and to St John's and back home again to Dublin, then up to Belfast. And, when he paid off with the rest of the crew, he couldn't wait to have a drink with his mates.

'Good God,' he said, taking his first mouthful of Guinness, 'but it's good to be back ashore for a while. I thought I wasn't gonna make it once or twice there, in the Western Ocean,' and he explained to them all about a deck cargo that shifted in a head sea, keeping an eye on the door in case his old man walked in.

Next trip he was a fireman, and he learned that the boiler pressure dictated the pace of the firing, and that firemen on a steamship poked the fire just as the housewife did, only the poker was called a slice.

The pressure gauge had to be around 210lb to the square inch, and when you were firing you weren't a hell of a lot better off than a trimmer, for the deck tilted in the stokehold just as it did in the bunkers. In addition, a heavy sea could – and often did – come in the fiddley or down the ventilators and douse the firemen in freezing cold water.

Salt tablets were on offer to make up for loss through sweat, but the old hands never took them. Instead, they sometimes added some porridge meal to their drinking water.

There was a marvellous camaraderie among the crews down below. If the firemen had a minute or two to spare they would give the trimmer a hand, and this was particularly so with a newcomer. They argued plenty, about football, boxing, books they had read, or places they had been, but it was rare indeed to see tempers lost.

They washed the coal dust out of their clothes with hot water from the exhaust tank in the stokehold. They scrubbed themselves clean after each watch. They kept their belongings stowed neatly and folded economically, for they were merchant seamen and they liked everything neat and tidy and shipshape.

In five years our young man had moved out of the stokehold into the engine room as a greaser. This was lighter work, but there was no slacking nevertheless. The engine room watches went as follows: twelve to four the greaser with the third engineer; four to eight the storekeeper with the second engineer; eight to twelve the donkeyman with the chief engineer and the fourth.

The chief stayed out of the engine room unless he was sent for, so the donkeyman was expected to make his experience available for the fourth engineer, who usually had no ticket.

All moving parts of the engine had to be oiled in a

continuous drill. Usually about forty minutes elapsed between oilings. As he squeezed the lubricant out of his oilcan, counting the drops to each part, the greaser felt the part with his hand, to check for overheating. The seven or eight parts in each leg of the triple expansion engine had to be oiled. The main thrust had to be felt for overheating even though it moved in a bath of oil. The six bearings along the shaft tunnel were oiled regularly, as part of the regime.

The ship's engines would use eighteen pints of oil a day if everything was normal, whilst in the stokehold the firemen were shifting forty-five tons of coal a day.

After about eight years our man was an old hand, signing on as storekeeper. All this meant was that he kept a tally of the engine room stores, paint, rags, brushes etc, and made up his books in port. Otherwise it was greasing whilst at sea, and on watch with the second engineer, at that – generally the second was regarded as a bit of a holy terror, responsible for the management of the engine room and stokehold crew.

He was married then, our storekeeper, and on the last day he was at home he would arrange for his wife to draw an advance of his fortnightly pay allotment. The advance note became payable when the ship left the coaling port or first loading port. This precaution was taken in case he jumped ship, for shipping companies couldn't afford a loss of the order of perhaps five pounds in the case of the one man in five thousand who might jump ship, you understand.

And there we'll leave him – as storekeeper. He no longer needed to make up stories for his pals about near shaves at sea. If you worked on the Western Ocean run the near shaves happened. You didn't need to make them up.

5

RACING FEVER

I don't know what other people will remember 1930 for but I will always remember it as the year our Jack started on the buses.

Jobs were extremely scarce then and Jim, Tommy and myself were still at school. The old man was ploughing the ocean (as Mother used to say, in her frequent dramatic moments) as donkeyman in the *Dunaff Head*, and Jack had been heaved out of Dixon's timber yard and was on the dole.

One day, like a bolt from the blue, the box clerk in the labour exchange sent Jack and a couple of others to Sandy Row bus depot and lo and behold he was taken on. The news went up and down Cosgrave Street like mad, for you have to remember that in those days to have a permanent and pensionable job was enough to lift you a rung above most in the locality.

Well, I'm telling you, that job started some fun in our house. Mother was terrified of Jack losing his 'good lovely job' as she called it. Everything and everybody in the house was in second place to Jack and his job. The Corporation put him on to what was called a spread. This meant rising at 6 a.m. and finishing about 9 p.m., with long, unpaid gaps in his duty through the day. It was the rising in the morning that caused the fun.

In the front bedroom Jack shared one bed with Mart. In the next bed was our Jim and me and on a mattress on the floor was Tommy. Before we got to sleep there was plenty of talking, and acting the goat, as you can imagine, between the five of us, with Mother shouting up the stairs at us to get to sleep.

'Jack, will you shut them'ns up an' git to sleep yerself,' she would yell. 'Ye'll niver be able to git up if ye don't,' and, in time – usually, I suppose, about half eleven – we would all be in the Land of Nod. Two hours, maybe three, would pass. We were all by that time really away out of this world, sending the snores up when –

Bang! The first sign was the crash of Mother's feet hitting the floor of the back room. Although she was low-set, she was no lightweight. When Mother jumped out of bed, every cup, saucer and windowpane in the house knew about it.

Bang! Thump, thump, thump! That was herself at the door of her own bedroom in three paces, with the first anguished cries reaching through the dark acres of sleep.

'Jack! Jack! God Almighty take care of us! Your good lovely job. Ye've slept in – ye've slept in. Get up! Get up! It's time to get up!' And on went the blinding light in our bedroom, to reveal Mother standing at the door in her shift, her eyes like saucers in panic, and Jack leaping out of bed in his shirt and into his trousers, still fast asleep.

Caught in the general pandemonium we would all sit up in bed and lend silent support to Jack, by this time probably falling off one leg to the floor, all tangled up in his trousers.

'I'll go down and make your breakfast. Hurry up, son!'
Mother would shout, and away she would go downstairs to
fry the bacon ends and dip bread without which no one in
our house was believed by Mother to be able even to
consider a day's work.

Jack would take the stairs three at a time in his hurry, and
we who remained would put the light out and get the old
heads down again, but within only minutes, Jack would be
back upstairs and the light would be on again.

'Two o'clock,' Jack would mutter to himself savagely.
'Two o'frigging clock.' Ripping his clothes off he would
hurl himself back into the scratcher, and the whole house
would try to get some sleep in, before Jack's real starting-
time came around.

The funny thing about all this was that Mother never felt
any shame about wrecking the routine of the house in this
way. 'Well,' she would say defiantly, 'it's better than sleepin'
in, isn't it?'

I suppose it was, really, but it didn't half jangle the nerves
all the same. Of course, Jack got the worst of it. There was
even a couple of times he found himself out in York Street
fully booted and spurred in his bus conductor's uniform,
giant-sized lunch wrapped up in brown paper and all, only
to learn that he was damn nearly one complete shift too
early for work.

Jack took it all very well, I must say. My nerves were so
jumpy that, if it had been me in his position, I would have
kipped down in the bus depot at nights, just to avoid the
wear and tear on the system.

It was round about this time too that our Mart got a
job at the dogs – Dunmore Park, that is, the greyhound

racing stadium. I remember it particularly because he used sometimes to bring home a loaf of brown bread that was meant for the greyhounds' grub. It was smashing too.

Mart walked No. 2 Blue and Kaiser Martin walked No. 1 Red. I can't remember who walked the other four dogs on the pre-race parades.

Although they gave up the practice later, in those days the track kept greyhounds in kennels on the premises. Mart and Kaiser Martin and the rest of the kennel boys had to walk these dogs for miles every morning. There was a kind of legend going in those times to the effect that Kaiser once wanted a particular dog to lose a race, and in order to make sure of it, he walked it sixteen miles to Ballyclare and back. Kaiser arrived back with badly blistered feet, but the greyhound enjoyed it so much that he won by half the track and nearly wrecked the track record as well. It might be true or it might not, but Kaiser Martin was certainly the sort of individual that kind of thing would have happened to, if it was going to happen at all. For example, he started up a football team once called North Star. A publican called McEldowney bought them their skip – red jerseys, white pants and red and white socks. After the team got settled into the league programme they appointed Kaiser Martin their manager and the first Saturday morning afterwards the team turned up at their home ground only to find that they had nothing to wear – Kaiser had pawned the skip.

Everybody and his uncle kept a greyhound at that time. All up and down the slopes of Cave Hill overlooking Belfast from the north there were bright-eyed optimists walking dogs. It must have been traumatic for the indigenous hare population.

Where on earth they got the stuff to feed their greyhounds heaven only knows, for, as I was saying, the loaves meant for the dogs at the track were sometimes knocked off for human consumption. Money for food was so scarce that kids like myself were sent down to John McCollum's bakery off York Street on a Monday morning to queue up for the bread and buns kept in the shop over the weekend. Stales, we used to call them, and in my case they were collected in a clean pillowcase, half filled for about a tanner.

Nearby McCollum's there was a pork store called Nathaniel Boyd's. Mother would have sent us there with a few pence for bacon bits. Sometimes the fellow behind the counter would have tossed in a fairly sizeable slice of good bacon or ham, without the boss's knowledge.

So how the devil they fed their greyhounds is a mystery, but they did. One chap in our street called Billy Bell acquired a greyhound which really looked the part. Black and white, I think it was, and it looked as if it was really some mover.

Going To Try it was called. It did a reasonable solo trial at the track and Billy Bell told everybody in the district to empty themselves on it, and so they did. Money was dug up from all directions and Cosgrave Street was heavily represented at Dunmore Park the night Going To Try made his debut.

He finished his race a strong last. Talk about a sickener. Forever afterwards that dog was referred to as Trying To Go. As far as I can recall it disappeared from human ken a short time after its one and only race. It was only but right that it should.

During the time he worked at Dunmore Park our Mart was an officer in the Church Lads' Brigade. I should have told you that, with the exception of Jack who got away with it because he was the oldest, and seeing the old man was away, the rest of us were up to the neck in the church, driven furiously to it by Mother. Tommy, Jim and I were in the robed choir and had to go out to the Sunday services wearing hard Eton collars and bow ties. Naturally we pulled our coat collars around them to hide them, but the other kids soon got to know about the bow ties and many a time we Macs had to sort some joker out on the way to church.

Sometimes, when I hear the voices of boy choristers in an echoing church I think of those times. Even though I felt hard done by, because of so many compulsory church services, nevertheless I used to love to be one of the choir, part of the magic sound formed when boys sing sacred music in the Lord's house.

But to get back to Mart. As an officer in the Church Lads' Brigade he went to camp with the boys a few months after he started working as a kennel-boy, and it wasn't long before he noticed a brave useful-looking greyhound being exercised in the area of the camp. After making friends with the owner, he found out the dog's name. It was called Let Paddy Cut. Mart told us about the dog and also advised us to start putting money by for its first appearance on the track.

Nobody did save up for it, of course, but it turned up at Dunmore Park all right a few months later and our whole family and connection put their faith in Mart, and shoved every juice they had on Let Paddy Cut.

He romped up at a very handsome price and our Jack bought a BSA bike out of the proceeds for £4. 19s. 6d.

There was another night when Mart either got a hold of some smashing information or else he was inspired, for he tipped five dogs out of seven and the whole five of them won. Mart signalled the number with the fingers of his left hand as he walked No. 2 Blue along the Tanner Straight. Watching him with eagle eyes were Uncle Alex, Aunt Lena's man, and Uncle Thomas. Alex took a nice profit after backing three winners and retired to the Hole in the Wall to celebrate, but Thomas the Lionheart trusted Mart to the end and made a fistful of dough.

But of course, with his weakness, the money did him more harm than good in the long run, for it only put him on the tear for days.

Having a big brother working in Dunmore Park gave me a certain advantage over the other kids in Cosgrave Street and district. I was allowed into the stadium the morning after a race meeting and could scavenge to my heart's content among the racegoers' flotsam in the stands. Cigarette cards were the big thing then, and I could have made up a couple of sets out of the empty packets left lying around by the punters. There was also an occasional sixpence or shilling to be found near the bookies' stands.

Those punters who were unable, for lack of the shilling admission fee, to take advantage of the noisy, colourful bookies inside the stadium were nevertheless catered for. Outside Dunmore Park, at the rear of the stand on the cheap side, a small group of 'penny bookies' used to operate.

A collaborator inside the stand would lean out of the

window yelling the odds and winners, whilst down below the penny bookies merrily laid bets, issuing numbered cloakroom tickets instead of the highly decorative tickets used by their wealthier brethren within the stadium.

It was one summer evening at this spot that I saw my first and only welsher. He was a stranger to the district who had unwisely laid a locally-owned outsider to a degree far in excess of his cash float. As soon as the number of the winning dog was announced he took off, sprinting as though from starting blocks, gaining a good fifty-yard start on his flabbergasted customers.

Whether the angry punters ever got their money I never did find out, but I would doubt it. That fellow had a pair of long legs that could fairly send him flying along, and when I last saw him he was leading the pack comfortably, heading up the hill towards the Antrim Road with probably the guts of fifty bob in his pocket and a good night's drinking ahead of him.

6
BACKGROUND
THE FINEST FIGHTING
MEN OF ALL

For the first half of the war the merchant seaman had the most dangerous job of any of the combatants, and he was the fighting man who was least appreciated by the press and public.

If any country other than Britain had been in the same debt to its merchant navy in 1940 the civilian seaman would have had the free run of the cities. But the British, as usual, chose to make heroes of the three uniformed arms. This at a time when the Royal Navy was signally failing to protect the merchant fleet, the Army had been flung out of Europe and the Royal Air Force bomber command had reluctantly only just given up dropping leaflets over Germany.

In March 1940, 107,000 tons of merchant shipping was lost. By April the total had risen to 158,000 and in May it went up to 288,000. June saw the half million mark passed easily, with 585,000 tons being sunk; in July and August the debit figure went down to just under 400,000 tons a month and September saw it rise again to 449,000 tons lost to the enemy at sea.

'The weakness of the British defences and escort forces are a great advantage to our submarines,' said a German Admiralty communiqué at the time.

When Churchill made his 'finest hour' speech to the Commons in June 1940 he did not even pay tribute to the merchant navy, though he did say that the country was sure of supplies and munitions of all kinds from the United States, without actually pointing out that the merchant navy was going to have to bring the supplies across the Atlantic at the cost of many thousands of sailors' lives.

Yet it is hard to find, in all the pages that have been written about the war, the name of a single merchant navy captain, officer or seaman that has lodged in the memories of the British people.

In the second half of 1940 the protection afforded the North Atlantic convoys was ludicrously insufficient. The anti-submarine forces, such as they were, were concentrated three hundred miles off the West of Ireland. For the whole of the journey from Canada or the USA to the Western Approaches a convoy was likely to be in the care only of an armed merchant cruiser. Yet to this day the picture that the public has of the war at sea is one in which a veritable fleet of frigates and destroyers protected the homebound ships, pouncing on the raiding submarines the moment they appeared.

Many graphic accounts have been written by U-boat sailors about the 'Happy Years' or the 'Years of Glory', when British merchant vessels were being sent to the bottom with comparative ease, and the early U-boat aces like Guenther Prien, who sank the battleship *Royal Oak* in

Scapa Flow in October 1939, were chalking up kills at an astronomic rate.

Those were the days when exultant U-boat crews were invited by their commanders to come forward, one at a time, to take a look through the periscope at the fat, rolling freighters, loaded to the Plimsoll Line, before the submarine surfaced in amongst the helpless targets, to slaughter them, sometimes three at a time.

The German submariners have described how, if they were astern of a large convoy, they would 'sniff' their way up to it by following the smell of smoke from the ships' funnels. It was all great fun.

In June 1940 U-boats sank the three armed merchant cruisers *Andania*, *Carinthia* and *Scotstoun*; in August the Armed Merchant Cruiser (AMC) *Transylvania* was torpedoed and in November the AMCs *Laurentic* and *Patroclus* were sunk by the U-boat ace Otto Kretschmer. Some of these AMCs were on Northern Patrol duty when sunk, but their loss nevertheless meant that the single AMCs escorting the North Atlantic convoys had less chance of being assisted in their work even by others of their own class.

Back in 1917 the British had learnt the vital lesson of the convoy system. In the five months from March to July of that year over two million gross tons of shipping were lost. These figures were considerably reduced when the convoys were formed.

When the Second World War broke out, however, the Admiralty seemed to have forgotten the lesson of 1917. Escorts were in very short supply, and many merchant vessels were instructed to make their way independently.

In 1939 Admiral Doenitz only had 26 submarines

capable of taking up station in the North Atlantic, and although only a third of these would have been on operations at any given time there were nevertheless over 2,000 British merchant ships at sea on any one day. By the end of 1939 the U-boats had sunk 102 ships which had been sailing independently and only 4 ships in convoy.

In asking ships' masters to take their vessels westward unescorted from a position one hundred miles out from Ireland the Admiralty overlooked the fact that the U-boats' range had increased dramatically since the First World War. As often as the British extended the limit of the area in which merchantmen were escorted westwards, so the submarines moved patiently further out into the Atlantic, and continued to fall upon the unprotected freighters after the British escorts had turned back homewards again.

The British Navy worked at a disadvantage in that they were deficient in knowledge regarding the behaviour of the ASDIC submarine detection equipment in deep-sea conditions and in conditions of extreme temperatures, or heavy marine traffic.

The Germans wrong-footed their enemy also by using the very simple, direct, yet totally unexpected tactic of attacking at night on the surface. All the Royal Navy's experience in the First World War had led them to believe that U-boat commanders were uncomfortable on the surface at any time and had a downright aversion to carrying out an attack on the surface against a protected convoy. Yet this is just what they did, and to extremely telling effect, at that. This meant that the ASDIC equipment was useless, since its value lay only in indicating underwater objects. For the first part of the war, the British, in the absence of effective radar, had to rely on ships' lookouts to detect submarines on the surface.

The fall of France in mid-1940 gave the U-boats a significant advantage. At one fell swoop it enabled Admiral Doenitz to establish submarine bases in the Biscay ports, thus shortening the distance from base to operational area by hundreds of miles.

The receptions given to victorious U-boats returning to bases like Lorient from duty in the North Atlantic in those days were almost hysterically enthusiastic. There were cheering crowds, brass band music and bouquets. The flotilla commandants and their staff stood at the salute as the travel-stained U-boats brought up their moorings. When the wolf-pack tactics were perfected in 1941 and it began to look as though the British lifeline was really breaking, the adulation for the U-boat crews was so great that even the French prostitutes from the many *établissements* in Lorient and Brest turned out in force at the quayside to greet the conquering heroes.

The first duty of a successful U-boat crew after landing was to attend a ceremonial dinner laid on by the base naval command. The meal was long and rich; champagne and local wine were drunk, and speeches of congratulations were made. Then the flushed crews were released, to find warm embraces from the French girls, and their first night in a comfortable bed for weeks. Afterwards the crew would be sent to the seaside resort of Carnac to rest and recuperate for a week. Here the tensed submariners lounged on the shore in the sunshine, swam with the dark French beauties, and danced and made love to them well into the night.

Meanwhile, across the water in Britain, the merchant seaman who was lucky enough to reach home after the terror-filled passage of the Western Ocean, was being frisked at the dock gates by harbour police, to make sure that he was not bringing home contraband, like a few ounces of tobacco, or – even worse – a couple of bottles of brandy. The customs men were sudden death on tobacco or drink.

Earlier in this chapter I pointed out that the average Britisher would be hard put to it to recall the name of a single merchant navy officer or seaman who had made a contribution in the war, yet names of soldiers, airmen and Royal Navy men still come tripping off the tongue without effort.

Here are two merchant navy names to fill the deficiency. No doubt, by the time another chapter has been read, these names, too, will have drifted back into oblivion.

Mr T.D. Finch (now Captain Finch), chief officer of the tanker *San Emiliano*, torpedoed at 9 p.m. on 6 August 1942, whilst carrying twelve thousand tons of high octane fuel out of Trinidad. He locked the door of his cabin against the horrific flames consuming his ship, climbed through the porthole to the shelter deck and made his way to the fo'c's'le head.

He threw himself on to the falls and slid into a boat while behind him flames were reaching a hundred foot high. Struggling to keep the boat clear of the burning sea, Finch and a handful of other survivors tried to help the horribly burned survivors in the sea. After watching several ship-mates in the boat die from their injuries, sail was hoisted and the lifeboat drifted away in the vast sea. Next day they were picked up by a US Army Transport. Seven men had survived out of a crew of forty-eight, but Mr Finch thinks that three of these were later lost in other ships. Certainly one of them – the radio officer – was.

Chief Engineer Charles Pollard, our second example, was one of sixteen of the forty-two-strong crew of the tanker *San Demetrio* who after abandoning their blazing ship when it was shelled by the pocket battleship *Admiral Scheer* on 5 November 1940 drifted down on the *San Demetrio* again in their lifeboat over a day later. Although the tanker was still ablaze, the men decided to try to sail their ship back home. They boarded the derelict vessel and fought the flames. Chief Engineer Pollard repaired the auxiliary boiler to run the pumps and they got the fires under control. On 8 November the chief engineer and his helpers got the main engines going, and on 13 November, with one of the sixteen dead and others badly hurt, they sailed the *San Demetrio* into Blacksod Bay, County Mayo, with most of its precious cargo intact.

There were thirty-two thousand merchant seamen from the Commonwealth lost in the war. All of them were volunteers. Every single one of them.

Thirty-two thousand lost out of 145,000. Beat that, Brigade of Guards, Long Range Desert Group, Paratroops, Marine Commandos, and Bomber Command!

No unit could approach the record of the British Mercantile Marine. They were the finest fighting men the world has ever seen. And hardly anybody, except their loved ones, knew it at the time.

7

MARRIOTT & SON

In 1934 Mart went to sea as a trimmer in the *Dunaff Head*. He was sailing shipmates with the old man, who had been donkeyman of this ship since 1924 without a break.

Needless to say it wasn't Mother's doing that Mart went away in the Head boat. Backs were to the wall, or she would never have gone along with any such outlandish idea. Mother regarded seamen as a feckless lot who gave too much of their hard-earned money to the publicans and didn't carry enough of it home. Of course this did not apply to Dad, who managed, in our eyes at least, to lend a great deal of dignity and style to the practice of celebrating his homecoming. In any case Dad brought most of his money in his allotment home and kept only his overtime earnings.

Mart had been eased out of Dunmore Stadium by the management, after looking for a handsome rise in pay. It was after this that Mr Topping, the headmaster of St Barnabas', employed him as a part-time coach for the school soccer team and someone in Henderson Avenue paid him for walking a greyhound on the Cave Hill. He was out of work for months, and he and I grew really close in this period.

Just to show how fiercely I loved him at that time I'll tell you about an incident that happened during a football match involving Mart's team, North Star. The game was being played at the Grove fields behind Dunmore Stadium. In those days of high unemployment it was quite common for a crowd of a couple of thousand to gather round the touchline for a junior league game involving a local side. It was free, and it was hard, exciting football. Mart, the team captain, was playing at right half.

Right beside where I stood on the touchline, the opposing left-winger, a dapper little chap, waltzed up to Mart and did a fancy little dance on either side of the ball, waving his hands at Mart and beckoning him to come and take it away from him. Much to his surprise the winger was unceremoniously grassed, and Mart blasted the ball about seventy yards diagonally across the field to get a good attack going.

About five minutes later the left-winger tried the same lark and got the same treatment – a hard but fair sliding tackle.

'That's a right dirty bastard,' a stranger on my left said, loudly. 'Try it on somebody your own size, ya blirt ye,' he yelled at Mart, through cupped hands, but Mart paid him no attention.

Meanwhile, I was sizing this guy up. I was boiling with rage. He was about thirty, a good twelve inches taller than I was and four or five stone heavier, which wasn't very remarkable, since I was usually called kipper hips, I was so skinny.

'Put that right half off, ref!' Loudmouth was yelling. I happened to look down at his feet.

Oh joy! Merciful God be good to me! He had a corn on his right foot. His shoe was slit to let it palpitate there in comfort.

'Ye dirty blirt ...' the barracker got out just before my size seven came down on his wee toe.

The shouted insult changed to an unbelieving scream. The stranger leapt right on to the field of play on one foot and then back into the crowd further along on the same foot. Then he sprang on to the field again, fell on one knee and began to keen, the way women do at a wake. He made to caress his split right shoe, couldn't bear to touch it, and settled, instead, for twitching along the playing pitch in a prone position, like a soldier looking for cover from the enemy. He was whinnying like a horse.

That, my friend, will teach you to shout insults to our Mart, I said to myself, as I made my way to the far side of the pitch. 'Come on North Star,' I yelled, in my boy's contralto, 'ye can ate them dirty blirts.'

For a short period at this time Mart had a job at McCue Dick's, the timber merchants. He got the sack for acting the goat and was mortified beyond all understanding when Mother took it on herself to go down to the foreman and plead on his behalf.

I can just imagine Mother fighting his case too. It would have been a mixture of supplication and fist-waving, with Mother one minute asking the foreman to give Mart one more chance and the next rolling her eyes and threatening to pull Mart limb from limb if he let the foreman down again. After he was back in McCue Dick's, of course.

Mart got the job back, but got the hammer again in a matter of days on purpose in order to satisfy his honour with his mates.

So then there was nothing for him but the sea.

And away he went with Dad on the *Dunaff Head*. And when I came back home after seeing them on board, I went quietly upstairs, closed the bedroom door, lay down on the bed, and cried like a baby, even though I was thirteen going on for fourteen.

I had never once cried for Dad going away. Yet I was seventeen years of age before I gave up crying every time Mart went away.

But I don't think anybody knew about it.

During the ten weeks that that first trip lasted I nearly drove Mother astray in the mind asking her where the boat was, when it would arrive at its next port, how long it would be there before it sailed for the next port after that, and when was Mart coming home. I wrote letters galore to Mart, addressing them to Mr Marriott McAughtry (Junior) on Mother's instructions. I sent Mart the crossword competitions from the *News of the World* – the one that he and I used to do together on Sundays, and when Mart eventually came home he told me, laughing, that I had forgotten to send the clues along with the puzzle.

When we kids wrote to Dad through the years we were under instructions to tell him how we were getting on at school and we had to set out a sample of the sort of sums we were being taught. When I first started this caper, even young as I was, I could never quite see the point in this since, naturally, I always picked a sum that I could easily manage, but it seemed to satisfy the old man anyway.

This wasn't the way I wrote to Mart though. When I sat down to write Mart a letter I had to work hard to keep the thing in reasonable bounds. I could have written him a letter as long as the *Belfast Telegraph*.

In my letters I told him everything. And I threw in a bit of comic relief every now and then, too, like telling him about the way the postman had warned me about the free samples, and the solicitor's letter …

I couldn't resist free sample offers, you see. It wasn't for the samples either. It was just to see my name and address on an envelope or package, neatly typed.

'Birley's Antacid Powder' it would say on the label, in big characters, then underneath: 'Captain S.J. McAughtry, 130 Cosgrave Street, Belfast, Northern Ireland, Ireland'.

Or: 'Weetabix' or 'Silvikrin Shampoo', followed by 'Captain S.J. McAughtry', etc!

One morning when the postman found me waiting, as expected, at the front door, he handed me the usual package. Then he stopped and wagged his finger at me: 'You cut this out now,' he said sternly.

'What?' I asked him, in a faint voice, for I knew very well what.

'This bloody Captain S.J. McAughtry business, that's what,' said the postman. 'You'll end up in bloody gaol, that's where you'll end up!'

I could only stare at him dumbly, as guilty as sin.

As if this wasn't bad enough, I began to get persistent letters from Silvikrin, asking me whether I had placed my order yet. This had not been anticipated at all and I really had no idea what to do about it. In fact it made me extremely nervous.

'You will recall,' wrote someone on behalf of Silvikrin, 'when sending for our sample recently, that you expressed interest in our lines. We note that we have not yet received your order ...' They seemed to think I owned a shop or something.

I hid two of the Silvikrin reminders up the chimney in the front bedroom over the fire that was never used, while I racked my brains for a way out of the trap that my hellish addiction to seeing my name in print had landed me into. Then one day I hit on the solution.

'What I did was,' I wrote to Mart, 'I sent a letter to Silvikrin on a page of my jotter saying, "I do not wish to place an order since I haven't even used up your sample yet, Captain S.J. McAughtry".'

'Then,' I told Mart, 'I wrote on a page torn out of Frankie Pattison's jotter, "Dear Sir, I am Captain S.J. McAughtry's Solicitor. Do not write any more letters to him or I will tell the police. Signed Captain Frankie Pattison". And that seems to have sickened Silvikrin.'

The years 1934 and 1935 were turning points in our family's fortunes. Tommy and Chattie had started work and Mart was making an allotment to Mother of, I suppose, about two or three pounds a month. Before we began to get on our feet, things were tight enough, though, because we were still having to pawn things occasionally.

Only Jim and I were still at school. Jim, for some reason, never had to do any pawning. I was the last of the line to carry out this hateful chore. Always on a Monday morning.

Monday mornings. Out of the front door holding the

parcel, wrapped in newspaper and thus a dead giveaway. Don't look round for God's sake. If you don't see yourself being seen going to the pawn then you haven't been seen.

Walk with the parcel under your left arm; tucked up inside your jacket. Try to hide it. Good Christ, but I hate this. How can the others laugh about it?

'There's a wee woman who lives in Arlington Street and so help me God she could pawn the dishcloth,' somebody in our family had said, and we had all roared with laughter. Well, it's easy to laugh when you're not doing it, isn't it?

Up to the top of Cosgrave Street and round the corner to the left. Good. Nobody about. It's only half eight. Too early for the mates to be on the street. Only a couple of men in dungarees at McBrien's corner. Casuals who couldn't get a day at the docks. They'll stand here at the corner for the rest of the day, maybe with a break to watch the trials at Dunmore.

Around the corner into Edlingham Street. Ernie's is over on the New Lodge Road. There's the whole of Edlingham Street to cover yet.

Pause. Switch the parcel to the other side, to keep it to the wall. Don't look around. Walk towards Duncairn Gardens. Keep your mind off the risk of being seen. Think. How much must you ask on the suit? 'Ask Ernie for fifteen shillings,' Mother had said, 'and take ten if he gives it.'

Nobody about. Keep going. Cover the parcel with your jacket. Walk sideways a bit. Ask for fifteen and take ten. This is worse than death.

'Hello Sam.' Christ!

Sweet Saviour! It's Jinny Hendry.

'Not talking to anybody?' For God's sake, Sam, say

something. Anything.

'Hello.' She's carrying a parcel too! Openly. In front of her. Shove yours further up your coat. This is like a frigging nightmare.

'Where are you going then?' She's so normal. Imagine normal.

'A message.'

'Where to?'

'Me Aunt Lily's.'

Jinny Hendry was my age. Insofar as I was prepared to give the odd millisecond of my thinking to girls I approved of her. She was brisk and matter-of-fact and she wasn't a poultice, like the other girls in our street.

'Going to yer Aunt Lily's? I know the Aunt Lily's you're going to.' There. Things can't get any worse. They can't get any worse than this.

'I *am* going to me Aunt Lily's. Definitely.'

'You're going to your kind uncle's, that's where you're going. Like me.'

Turn and look at her. Look at her full in the face for the first time. You might as well. Things actually *have* got worse. She's actually prepared to openly discuss going to the pawn. Beat that! Whenever you get back from a pawning expedition, Mother always asks did anybody see you and you always assure her no. Well, boy, is the old woman in for a shock this morning. Did anybody see me? You bet somebody saw me. Jinny Hendry saw me and we walked to the pawn together, so we did. Talk about people seeing me!

'I hate going here,' you confess to Jinny.

'So do I but it has to be done,' she says. Looking at you, smiling at your embarrassment.

And in no time at all, by some miracle, you and Jinny are walking, relaxed and easily to the pawn. You're not even hiding the parcel.

You tell Jinny about the wee woman from Arlington Street who can pawn the dishcloth, and as you both turn into Ernie's doorway, Jinny Hendry's clear laughter is left behind, to echo in the quiet street, on a dull Monday morning.

The waiting is over and Mart is home from his first trip. I ran down the street to meet him. Ten yards away I stopped. I couldn't believe my eyes.

What did they do to you? He looks like death. His eyes are sunken, and his face is like a skull.

'Oh, I was desperate seasick,' he told me, smiling. 'But I got over it coming home.' His arm around my shoulder, we walked up the street. Mother bit her lip at the sight of him. 'Was it bad son?' she wanted to know.

'It wasn't too hot at first,' Mart said cheerfully, 'but I'll be all right when I get a charge of your stew into me,' and he gave her a big hug, and winked at me over her shoulder with his poor sunken wreck of a face.

As I sat beside him on the sofa, helping him to unpack his bag, I suddenly grabbed his hand, and turned it over, palm upwards. The whole palm of his hand was calloused, and pitted in a hundred places with black coal specks that were permanent, like tattoos. I looked up at Mart.

He smiled at me. 'I've got real sailors' hands now,' he said.

That's one of the things the Head Line gave you for nine pounds a month. Real sailors' hands.

8

BACKGROUND

A CHRONICLE OF 1940

Here is a potted chronicle of the year 1940, just to give the reader the flavour of the time.

Britain commenced the year having notched up nine U-boat sinkings in the four months of 1939 that the war had lasted. In the whole of 1940 a further twenty-two U-boats were to be sunk. The long-term production plan for the German Navy called for fifty-two Atlantic submarines and thirty-two coastal versions to be built in the year, so the British had a debit balance in terms of submarine sinkings during 1940.

The great German submarine aces managed to live through 1940. Gunther Prien, who had successfully penetrated Scapa Flow in October 1939 and sunk the battleship *Royal Oak*, was terrorising the sea-lanes, as was Otto Kretschmer, the greatest of them all. Kretschmer was eventually captured in March 1941 when his boat, U-99, was blown to the surface by depth charges and shelled into submission.

By July 1940 Prien was in the final stages of a personal challenge match with his former watch officer on the Scapa Flow voyage, Engelbert Endrass. Endrass had returned from patrol in the U-46 having sunk 35,000 tons of shipping, including the AMC *Corinthia*, and Prien had only one torpedo left and was well behind his former subordinate's total. He dramatically beat Endrass' score in the North Channel when, on top of his other kills on the trip, his boat U-47 torpedoed and sank the *Arandora Star*, 15,500 tons.

Neither Prien nor his cheering crew knew at the time, however, that the *Arandora Star* was carrying German and Italian civilian internees to Canada when she was torpedoed. Many of Prien's compatriots' lives were lost in this sinking. Prien himself was to die at the bottom of the sea with the rest of his crew in March 1941.

By 31 August 1940 the big ships *Scharnhorst*, *Gneisenau* and *Lutzow* were in Kiel refitting, the *Hipper* was in dock in Wilhelmshaven and the *Admiral Scheer* was in Danzig, working up for a voyage in late October.

In February 1940 seventeen German destroyers were engaged in laying mines, undetected, right on Britain's doorstep, off Newcastle, the Humber, Cromer and the Thames Estuary.

Back in November 1939, luckily for the British merchant fleet, observers near Shoeburyness had spotted an inept German pilot float two mines by parachute on to the mud flats instead of the deeper water beyond. Royal Navy mine specialists went out to take a look at them – and Britain had found the secret of the magnetic mine.

Still in February, another German pilot, even more inept, mistook German destroyers for British and sank two of them, the *Leberecht Maas* and the *Max Schultz* in the North Sea. Five hundred and seventy-eight German sailors were lost. A court of enquiry found that it was nobody's fault.

On 30 July 1940 Admiral Somerville eliminated the French fleet at Oran.

In September 1940 came the first operational test of the wolf-pack tactics. The rules of this manoeuvre were that the first U-boat to sight a convoy called up HQ, who would then direct further U-boats to the spot. Convoy SC 2 out of Sydney, Nova Scotia, was the first of many lumbering processions of merchantmen to be attacked in this way. Comprising fifty-three vessels, the convoy was nearing its escorts in the Western Approaches on 6 September without knowing that the enemy had decoded the rendezvous signal and had sent the U-boats 65, 28, 47 and 99 to meet the ships as well – the last two commanded by Prien and Kretschmer respectively. The attack lasted several days and nights and cost the convoy five ships – not much on the face of it, but the first indication of the maulings that awaited the hitherto unscathed Atlantic convoys. Only a couple of weeks later, on 20 September, an HX Convoy from Halifax, Nova Scotia, got the same treatment. Numbered HX 72 this convoy lost twelve ships out of forty-one. Gunther Prien in U-47 had been the scout who had called the others to the attack. Another great ace, Joachim Schepke, torpedoed seven of these ships himself in the U-100. October brought the wolf packs their juiciest pickings. Within five days, from 15 to 20 October, no fewer than forty-two ships were sunk in four different convoys. The convoy to suffer most was SC 7, comprising thirty-four ships. Only thirteen of these vessels reached port safely in Britain. The champagne flowed in Lorient after that one.

Meanwhile, what was the general public being told about

the war in 1940? Here are some of the stories that reached the papers:

'Will Hitler try to bombard London?' ran one headline in February 1940. The item dealt with a report that Hitler had a gun with a range of over 150 miles. A well-drawn sketch showed the gun located on the Dutch island of Walcheren, firing shells which travelled through the stratosphere on their way to London.

'Fantastic as such a suggestion may be it cannot be contemptuously brushed aside as just another attempt to make our flesh creep ...' the author said, in a rare moment of prescience, bearing in mind the V2 rockets that fell on London in 1944. However, he spoiled the effect later in the article. When dealing with the chances of the giant gun being sited on Walcheren, he said: 'Though twice menaced already, Holland is still inviolate, and in the opinion of most good judges, likely to remain so.'

On the subject of the arming of merchant ships, Mr Churchill, First Lord of the Admiralty, told the Commons at the beginning of the year: 'We have already armed more than one thousand merchant ships for self-defensive purposes and the process is continuing with all possible speed. It will not be long before we have two thousand so armed. These merchant ships, in accordance with the oldest rights of the sea, fire back when they are attacked. The merchant captains and seamen show a resolute disposition to defend themselves and many duels are fought in which the U-boat, fearing to be damaged and thus be unable to dive or attack, is beaten off.'

The premier, Mr Chamberlain, referred to the Navy as 'the first line of defence of these islands, and of that great

Empire which was built up by the toil and the enterprise of our forefathers.'

Only four months later Chamberlain (forefathers or no forefathers!) argued, together with Lord Halifax, the foreign secretary, that Britain should give Mussolini Malta and other British colonies in return for his promise to get acceptable peace terms for Britain from Hitler. But nobody outside the Cabinet was to know that for a very long time.

The first Australian contingent bound for the Western Front marched up Martin Place, Sydney, and got their pictures in the paper in February. Around about this time the first German bomber to crash in England came down in Yorkshire, killing two of the crew. Mr George Jackson of Whitley Urban Council was there to see it and to talk to the press about it.

It was a Heinkel. The survivors were given cigarettes and a cup of tea by a Miss Smales, who lived in a nearby farm.

'Will it always be quiet on the Western Front?' ran a headline in March 1940. 'Nowhere else but on the Western Front, argue many military authorities, is a really decisive issue possible,' the article said. But the author disagreed with the military authorities.

'Well may we believe,' he wrote, 'that Hitler will choose anywhere but here for his Blitzkreig – here, where millions of men lie entrenched around the thickly-massed guns.'

In May 1940 Norway was being bombed by the RAF. The public were being assured that our arms were having considerable success there, following the German invasion. Pictures appeared in the press of bombed harbours and ravaged towns by the fjords, and maps of Norway were profuse.

The German invasion of Denmark was a fait accompli and the papers were explaining that the occupation of Denmark was a necessary preliminary to the attack on Norway.

Our submarines were busy off Norway. The crews of the *Sealion*, the *Snapper* and the *Sunfish* were shown relaxing after actions in which forty thousand tons of German shipping were claimed sunk.

The battleship *Warspite* sank seven German destroyers in the second battle of Narvik and action shots appeared in May 1940.

The Dutch were getting worried about the increasing activity of fifth-columnists and the Dutch Government felt it necessary to issue a statement about it: 'Holland lies in a storm-cone of Europe and it is necessary to take the greatest precautions ...'

In June there were pictures of wounded Belgian soldiers arriving in England. British readers were being told that German motorcycle units were a surprise element in the German advance in Europe. 'Leopold Opened the Gate to the Enemy' told all as far as the fall of Belgium was concerned.

The RAF were on the eve of their greatest triumphs in the Battle of Britain but their deeds in the European theatre were being extolled too. 'Whenever the RAF met the Germans in fair fight,' wrote Air Marshal Sir Phillip B. Joubert de la Ferte, 'that is, one British aeroplane to three or four Germans, the victory was on our side.'

'Will Hitler Come with a Fleet of Barges?' they were asking in August. 'There are too many "ifs"' wrote one prophet: 'If the weather were fine and the sea fairly calm. If the British Navy were temporarily or permanently out of the picture. If the Germans had superiority in the air. If they had a reasonable share of Hitler's customary luck – then the passage across the narrow seas might be made. But there are altogether too many ifs.'

As far as German air superiority was concerned, Hermann Goering found out between 12 August and 15 September 1940 that he could not keep his promise to Hitler and wipe out Fighter Command in time for the invasion of Britain in mid-September.

Radar, radio and self-sealing petrol tanks were surprise bonuses for the RAF in the Battle of Britain. By 26 August the Luftwaffe had lost 602 fighters and bombers and the RAF had lost 259 fighters. In the first week of September Goering came very close to success, bringing down 185 British aircraft for the loss of 225 German machines.

At this point Hitler ordered the bombing of London and the RAF breathed again. London was badly damaged but the main targets – the radar and fighter stations were allowed to recover their efficiency.

The final action in the Battle of Britain took place on 15 September when two successive waves of bombers with fighter cover were mauled. After this Hitler shelved his plans to invade England.

By the end of 1940 Mussolini's forces were being knocked about by the Greeks in Albania, and Coventry went into action to clear its bomb damage.

King George VI toured Southampton in December accompanied by Mr Herbert Morrison and an army of local dignitaries. Bristol was licking her wounds after heavy air raids and the Minister of Labour was expressing concern because of the shortage of labour for munitions factories.

An official Air Ministry communiqué revealed that the RAF had bombed naval bases at Bremen, Bremerhaven, Hamburg, Kiel and Wilhelmshaven.

Kiel had been bombed six times during November, the Air Ministry pointed out – on the 3rd, 10th, 15th, 19th, 25th and 28th.

But all of these air raids came too late to stop the battleship *Admiral Scheer*. She had passed through the Kiel canal at the end of October. By the middle of December 1940 she was oiling from the supply ship *Nordmark* in the South Atlantic, just north of the Equator.

In the last two weeks of 1940 the German naval ratings on the *Scheer* were beginning to think of Christmas. They had had a busy time since sailing from Kiel. The 150 prisoners from the British vessels *Port Hobart*, *Tribesman* and *Mopan*, just transferred to the *Nordmark*, were proof enough of that.

Already the wreckage of the *Jervis Bay*, the *Kenbane Head* and four other ships of her convoy, sunk by the *Scheer* on 5 November 1940 halfway across the North Atlantic convoy route from Halifax to Britain, was beginning to rust on the seabed.

9

WE ALL MOVE HOUSE

From 1935 onwards the *Dunaff Head* ran nice and regularly to Canada and back every two months. Dad was a fixture on this ship, like the funnel, and Mart was becoming one as well. He was a fireman until 1936, when he went into the engine room as a greaser. Mart was very pleased with this move, for Dad tended to be very hard on him at sea. On separate watches in the engine room at least they spent more time apart.

Why on earth Dad had to be like that used to baffle me, for although Mart was always fond of larking about in a physical sort of way – one playful dig from him and you were paralysed for an hour, for he didn't know his own strength – nevertheless he was a very conscientious fellow.

Well, you could tell. He never missed church when he was at home. He didn't drink, except maybe to take an odd shandy. He didn't swear, except occasionally when one of his heavier bets on the horses got the hammer, and nearly anybody would do that.

Strangely enough he didn't pay much attention to the girls, although there were enough of them interested in him around the church and that. He was very good-looking when he was dressed up, our Mart. Through sailing to places like Montreal and Quebec in the summertime he was as brown as a nut, and his teeth were white and strong. A lock of dark hair used to fall over his eye sometimes, and occasionally, sitting by Mart in church, I used to look sideways at him and think how smashing he looked, in his navy blue suit and white shirt, sunburnt face and good white teeth. I was all delighted, too, when I noticed the girls with their eye on him, but one way and another, Mart was far more interested in football and boxing and backing a horse or a dog now and again, than he was in the ladies.

So why the old man should want to go hard on him at sea, I don't know, for Mart must have been a powerful rarity among seamen – a practically teetotal churchgoer who left the girls alone. You wouldn't have got my old man inside a church, you know. Not for a crate of John Jameson's you wouldn't. So there wasn't any need for him to be so strict with Mart.

Mother and Dad were in powerful contrast in this church business. We in the family used to agree between ourselves that Mother was next door to a religious fanatic. Here's what I had to go through, for example, on the Lord's Day, on the first Sunday of the month:

8.00 a.m.	Holy Communion with rumbling stomach. It was a sin to eat before it. Manna from heaven afterwards in the shape of fried bacon and dipped bread.
10.00 a.m.	Morning Sunday School. Our woman teacher was painfully shy. I used to make her even shyer by asking, for example, whether Mary Magdalene wore lipstick.

11.30 a.m.	Morning Service. Tommy, Jim and I sang in the robed choir.
3.00 p.m.	Afternoon Sunday School. I fiddled the collection here, so that I had three pence for the 8pm banker school at Canning Street corner.
4.00 p.m.	Church Brotherhood Service. Men only. Robed choir in attendance and sermons calculated to interest men. Example: the component parts of a flower and how the whole lot worked as a unit to the glory of God and William Wordsworth.
7.00 p.m.	Evening Service. Robed choir in attendance. All I can remember of this, apart from a lasting love for the sound of wind and rain on old church timbers, is that I sat in the choir stalls beside a boy from the Limestone Road whose breath was stinking.

In addition to this lot we were expected to turn up at any event run by the church through the week, and Tommy, Jim and I were cornerstones in the Church Lads' Brigade, while Chattie was at first a member, then an old girl, of the Girls' Life Brigade.

I could never quite figure out whether Mother hurled herself and us into Christianity with such vigour because she wanted to insulate herself from Dad's cheerful godlessness, or whether, in the absence of Dad from the usual position as head of the house, she felt that the Lord wouldn't be a bad substitute in the job.

At the beginning of 1935 changes took place in regard to our home addresses, not all of them pleasant. To begin with, Mother decided to leave Cosgrave Street and take a bigger house in Hillman Street with parlour, kitchen, scullery, three bedrooms – and a bathroom, if you please.

This was a pleasant change, and one that was long overdue, but when Uncle Thomas and Uncle James had to move it wasn't so good – especially in the case of Uncle Thomas.

I should explain here that there was a periodic upsurge of feeling against the Catholics in the mid-1930s, including a bit of the usual burning-out of homes. Uncle Thomas was a Catholic; his turn came around in 1935 and so the house in which he lived alone on Collyer Street – the house where my grandmother's picture hung on the wall – was subjected to a ritual burning.

Not very much of a burning mind you, for he was liked in the district for his generosity, and pitied for his self-destroying alcoholism. The neighbours contented themselves by pouring some paraffin on the white scrubbed kitchen table and setting fire to it. There was so little else in the room that it was easy to restrict the flames to the table and leave it at that.

As it happens, I was mooning on my own as usual – in nearby Osborne Street – when the word spread that somebody was being burnt out in Collyer Street.

Happy and excited at this unexpected diversion, I challenged a couple of kids from the Limestone Road and the three of us set off neck and neck to see who would get to the burning first.

I couldn't believe my eyes when I saw that the knot of perhaps fifty people were actually clustered outside Uncle Thomas's house. I couldn't take it in, when I realised that the thin veil of smoke that wreathed through the broken front window meant that it was Uncle Thomas who was being told to go.

Such a burning was always timed to happen when the Catholic residents were out. The idea was to deliver a warning: they were not meant to return to that address again.

I must have looked pretty stupid, standing there at the edge of the crowd, watching Uncle Thomas's house burn and listening to the Orange songs being sung in thin, reedy voices by the crowd. Actually there was nothing at all going on in my head at the time. All the reasoning and judgement processes were arrested. I could only stand and watch dully, uncomprehending.

Suddenly a boy of my own age from somewhere in Tiger's Bay pointed to me and nudged a couple of companions. 'He must be one, too,' he shouted, 'that's his uncle's house.'

'I'm not!' I said angrily. 'I'm not one.'

Nor indeed was I 'one'! The truth of the matter was that my mother's parents were mixed and the practice at the time they were married – around 1885 – was that the religion of the children depended on their sex: if the father was Catholic, the boys were Catholic. This was the case in my mother's family, so Mother, Aunt Lena and Aunt Berry were Church of Ireland and Uncle Thomas, James, Sammy and Hugh were not.

Mixed marriages were widespread then, and the effects had widespread acceptance and understanding. So when the boy in the crowd pointed the finger at me, the rest of the crowd paid hardly any heed. Doubtless many of them didn't want too much attention paid to this aspect of the matter because of complications in their own background.

My mother and Aunt Lena were Protestants who had

married Protestants, so their children had Protestant parents. Thus the conditions for membership of the Orange Order were satisfied and indeed I was one day to see an Orange banner resting outside my own home in Hillman Street, and my mother making sandwiches and pouring Guinness for the bandsmen on Easter Tuesday, when my brother Jim, as Worshipful Master, led his lodge off on the Juvenile Orange annual march.

But Uncle Thomas had to leave Collyer Street for good, and a colourful chapter in our family story was closed. Thomas was never again to lead the kids of Tiger's Bay in singing hymns to aggravate his Salvation Army neighbours, and he would never call into our house in his noisy, bantering style any more. The pigeons would wait in vain to be fed by him, on the cobblestones of Collyer Street.

He went to live permanently in Carrick House, a Corporation hostel in Carrick Hill largely used by down-and-outs, and although we would see him around York Street occasionally, Uncle Thomas withdrew into himself after the burning and he was never the same, lively man again. He just lived for the bottle and went to hell headlong, as his tolerant neighbours who were in the Salvation Army used to put it.

Uncle James, too, decided to leave his little house in Mackey Street and go to live on the west side of the city after the burning, although his house was left alone and on the face of it he was getting on all right with his neighbours. Of course James was a totally different character to Thomas, his brother. James could take a drink or leave it. He was also a neat dresser who liked to have things nice and shipshape about his house, and that, but even so he was a colourful enough character in those days.

I shall remember Uncle James above all else for the way in which he fashioned the spoken word into something rich and wholly enjoyable. His style of speech was particularly noticeable because of the contrast it provided to my father's.

Dad was dry; a man of one word, where one would do. I found when I was very young that he tended to reduce my natural excitability and rapid-fire speech delivery to something approaching his own slower pace by the way in which he would listen gravely to the opening burst of my story. Before I had spoken to Dad for very long, I would find myself slowing down and wondering why I had thought the topic worthy of mention in the first place.

I didn't see a lot of Uncle James when I was a youngster. Remaining single until he was in his fifties, he was very much a man's man and didn't spend a lot of time visiting around his married sisters, but when he did listen to one of us kids telling a tale, he listened beautifully.

Like the rest of his family, he was a small man. His hair was dark and bushy and his black eyebrows set off a face that would have had any artist reaching for his sketch pad. Uncle James's wonderfully lively features seemed to be constantly changing. A muscle at his jaw was working as he clenched and unclenched his teeth and his mouth with its long upper lip was never at rest; either it was recovering from a laugh or else working up to a laugh or perhaps his lips would be writhing in an exaggerated snarl as he talked of something that had annoyed him.

When he was amused Uncle James's whole face and speech reflected it, and the laughter bubbled through every word that he spoke. When he was retailing a funny story he had to have two or three tries before he got the punchline out, so broken up with laughter did his words become.

But when he talked of his annoyance, his eyes became wild, he clenched his fists and waved them and the spit formed on his lips. Uncle James gave the impression of considerable strength, despite his small size. I rarely saw him freshly angered, but I saw him many times relive his anger at earlier experiences and it was enough to make me wonder at the force of the real thing, when it possessed him. Certainly he was capable of explosive violence when pushed, for he had turned on Uncle Thomas, his brother, once, when the latter went too far with his needling, and with one punch put him into the Mater Hospital with a couple of cracked ribs.

His oaths were marvellous. I loved to hear him swear, although in our house, he wasn't allowed to go very far before Mother pulled him up.

'Sweet Saviour Christ, Lizzie, but that gut of mine's murdering me the day,' he would say, entering the house, his eyes rolling. 'That curse-o'-God indigestion again.'

'Not, so help me, Christ, till God calls me, will I ever forget the pain o' that bloody stummick this day,' he would say, holding his hand across his stomach and leaning almost drunkenly against the kitchen door, the better to let all those inside see the extent of his anguish.

I must admit I picked one or two of his habits up myself in this direction, and I've had a good few tickings off for it, like himself.

He loved children and would not only listen interestedly to their chattering but would chime in wherever he could to help the story along. We kids could never see enough of him. For my part I was sorry that Uncle James's visits to our house were so rare in those days. Not only was he a joy to talk to – he was an absolute delight to listen to. I still remember well one of the stories he used to love to leave us with at the end of a visit.

Two old ladies were at the music hall, sitting in a box, listening to the orchestra play. When the performance finished, one old lady turned to the other: 'What lovely music, Mary,' she said, 'I wonder what it's called.'

The other old girl shook her head. 'I'm afraid I don't know, Martha,' she said, 'but there's a card down there at the side of the stage. Maybe that'll tell us. I'll just turn my opera glasses on it.' She peered for a while through her glasses.

Then she turned to her companion with a puzzled expression on her face.

'That's a queer name for a piece of music, Martha,' she said.

'Why, what's it called?' Martha asked.

'It's called the Refrain from Spitting,' she said.

10

PRELUDE TO THE SLAUGHTER I
THE *JERVIS BAY*

In 1793 Sir John Jervis, in command of a fleet of fifteen British warships, engaged and destroyed twenty-seven Spanish men-of-war near Cape St Vincent. Sir John's most brilliant and courageous captain in this action was one Horatio Nelson, but it was to the fleet commander that the honours went and one such honour was to have a bay, eighty miles south of Sydney, Australia, named after him.

When the Australian Government Commonwealth Line ordered a new passenger liner from Vickers in 1922 it was policy that the ship would be named after an Australian bay; she was called *Jervis Bay* and joined her sister-ships *Esperance Bay*, *Hobson's Bay*, *Largs Bay* and *Moreton Bay*.

The First World War had ended less than four years earlier, so the memory of the mauling that the Allied naval and merchant fleet had received at the hands of the Germans was still fresh in the minds of the Admiralty. Accordingly the Australian Government agreed to have the *Jervis Bay* constructed to heavier-than-usual standards so that, if need be, she could convert easily to the role of armed merchant cruiser.

She was a vessel of 13,839 tons, managed by 15 officers

and 164 men. Her average passenger complement was 600, sailing in one-class accommodation.

But the five-ship fleet was incurring heavy losses and all the vessels were sold to the Aberdeen and Commonwealth Line in 1928. *Jervis Bay* was the last to be transferred.

The *Bay* ships sailed between England and Australia, carrying emigrants to a new land and fresh horizons, and bringing Australians back on holiday for what was often their first glimpse of the old country. Industrial products were carried on the outward voyage, and wool, meat, fruit and wines were brought back from Australia.

The *Jervis Bay* was not an elegant ship. She was just a solid, workman-like liner, doing a routine job. Since the new owners paid the low British merchant marine wages, the *Bay* ships had been converted to profit-makers, running a regular service from Southampton to Brisbane, Sydney, Melbourne, Adelaide and Fremantle.

So the *Jervis Bay* plodded back and forth to Australia for another eleven years until, in August 1939, when she was seventeen years old, the Admiralty looked up their dusty records, learned that she had been earmarked for duty as an armed merchant cruiser, and requisitioned her for service. The war was just around the corner.

'Cruiser' was a singularly inappropriate term to apply to a passenger liner which had been converted for wartime naval use. A real cruiser was a purpose-built fighting machine, sleek and fast, with a low silhouette, and packed almost to bursting point with lethal weapons and aids to their efficient use. Cruisers could pulverise harbours and claw attacking bombers from the sky with 80mm, 40mm and 20mm automatic weapons. They could and did shadow and harass battleships; cruisers could and did cause one battleship – the *Graf Spee* – to be scuttled in ignominy, after three of them had severely damaged it.

The *Jervis Bay* and her sort by contrast were elderly passenger ships, and despite strengthened construction to Navy specifications at the time they were built, their hulls and bulkheads might as well have been made of balsa wood, so useless were they against high-velocity naval artillery.

The *Jervis Bay* sat high in the water, her funnel and superstructure a complete giveaway on the horizon. Anything less like a cruiser would be difficult to imagine. And as for her armament – this amounted to seven 6-inch guns cast at the end of the nineteenth century, and two anti-aircraft guns that were not much younger. The effective range of the main armament was ten to twelve thousand yards. All seven guns were worn and inaccurate.

The Navy did not, of course, propose to employ the AMCs on the full range of duties of a cruiser. Instead they were to be used on convoy escort duties, and on contraband searches on the Northern Patrol in the Denmark Strait, between Greenland and Iceland.

Contraband control was an essential measure in the blockade of Germany. In her attempt to throttle the German economy it was necessary for Britain to cut off supplies to the enemy ports by intercepting enemy and neutral shipping bound for those ports. Armed merchant cruisers had carried out Northern Patrol duties splendidly in the First World War and, despite Admiralty insistence that conventional cruisers were needed for this work, the politicians had decided to make naval savings by relying on the AMCs in the event of the outbreak of another war with Germany.

It had been intended that the *Jervis Bay* should be used on the Northern Patrol shortly after hostilities were declared. She had been fitted out for war, which is to say that a primitive form of fire-control, gun drill and ammunition-handling had been devised for her, and by late November 1939 she was based at Scapa Flow with a crew of naval reservists, ready to commence blockading the enemy.

But at the last minute the *Jervis Bay* damaged her windlass and had to go to the Tyne for repairs. Because of this her place on the Northern Patrol was filled by another AMC – the *Rawalpindi*, the first AMC in the Second World War to be engaged by enemy surface forces.

The *Rawalpindi*, a former P&O liner, of 16,700 tons, had been running to ports in the Far East before being requisitioned by the Admiralty as an AMC: she was commanded on patrol by a Royal Navy man, brought back from retirement at sixty, Captain Edward C. Kennedy. Halfway through the afternoon watch on 23 November, when the war was just fifty days old, the *Rawalpindi* was on station between the Faroes and Iceland. Suddenly an ominous, dark silhouette appeared on the horizon, closing rapidly. Soon the identity of the stranger was beyond dispute. She was the battle cruiser *Scharnhorst*.

Capable of twenty-nine knots, carrying nine 11-inch guns, twelve 5–9-inch guns, and formidably armour-plated, the *Scharnhorst* would have been a tough proposition for any two British cruisers: for the *Rawalpindi* the encounter was a catastrophe.

When she was three miles from the AMC the *Scharnhorst*

turned on to a parallel course and signalled to the *Rawalpindi* to heave to.

Instead, Captain Kennedy ordered a turn to port and the *Rawalpindi* headed for a patch of fog at full speed.

Scharnhorst immediately turned on to an intercepting course and increased speed.

Kennedy decided by way of evasive action to make for a large area of ice to starboard but, as the *Rawalpindi* turned, the *Scharnhorst* sent a shell into the sea just ahead of her. The signal to heave to was repeated.

At that moment the lookout reported a second stranger to starboard – a cruiser.

Soon she, too, was close enough for identification. It was the *Gneisenau*, sister-ship of the *Scharnhorst*.

The *Rawalpindi* was now finished for certain – opposing her were the two biggest and best ships in the German Navy. The stage was set for a slaughtering match.

'Abandon your ship,' the *Scharnhorst* signalled. Kennedy maintained her course and speed.

Twice more the *Scharnhorst* ordered the British crew to abandon ship. *Rawalpindi*, at the moment of receiving the third order, opened fire on *Gneisenau* and hit her amidships. A salvo aimed at *Scharnhorst* fell short.

Both German warships then turned their guns on the *Rawalpindi*. The first salvo wiped out the main fire control position, put one of the starboard guns out of action and killed most of those on the bridge of the AMC. Further hits knocked the power supply out and set the plentiful woodwork in the liner ablaze.

Captain Kennedy set off towards the after section of the ship to arrange the laying of a smokescreen, but on the way he was killed by a bursting shell. There were now dead and wounded in all sections of the *Rawalpindi*, but she still managed to keep a few guns firing, although the ammunition had to be manhandled from the magazine.

Suddenly the forward magazine was hit. The *Rawalpindi* broke in two and the battle was over. From first-sighting to final destruction it had taken an hour and a half.

The two German warships picked up twenty-seven survivors immediately after the action, and eleven more were rescued next day by another AMC, the *Chitral*.

Back home in London, ten of the survivors, hatless and in borrowed clothing, were inspected on Horse Guards Parade by Admiral Sir Charles Little, Chief of Naval Personnel.

In the Commons Neville Chamberlain said: 'These men must have known as soon as they sighted their enemy that there was no chance for them, but they had no thought of surrender. They fought their guns until they could be fought no longer. Many of them went to their deaths carrying on the great traditions of the Royal Navy. Their example will be an inspiration to others.'

Captain Kennedy and 238 of his men lost their lives in this one-sided action.

The naval warrior has a much heavier burden to bear in battle than his comrades in the army. The soldier can honourably raise his hands when his situation is hopeless, and approach the foe with his life intact. For the naval combatant surrender is only possible when his ship has been shot from under him.

If a captain were to surrender his ship and crew because his situation was tactically hopeless then nothing is surer than that he would be court-martialled when the gates of the prison camp eventually opened to let him out.

All that remained then for the British – or for that matter the German – fighting sailor when confronted by over-whelming odds was to go along with the myth that he was dying for a tradition, and that he had a choice in the matter.

In fact the choice had already been made for him. By the Admiralty and the Government and every man, woman and child of the British public. 'Surrender, for the sailor whose ship is intact, is a disgrace,' they say.

'But,' they tell him, 'when you die in the killing match. Then … then, we'll make you a hero. And your name will live forever …'

Back on the Tyneside the men of the *Jervis Bay* read about the death of the *Rawalpindi*, and reflected on the trick of fate that had put Kennedy and his crew on to the *Jervis Bay*'s patrol.

If this were to happen to their ship, they thought, they would have to travel the same one-way route. And the politicians and the Admiralty, the journalists and the historians would all play out the same farce – the pretence that they had had a choice in whether or not they lived, or whether their bodies would be shredded by high explosive, or burned to roast beef, or become bloated and pale grey by drowning.

The *Jervis Bay* had her refit and sailed from the Tyne – not to the Northern Patrol after all, but to convoy escort duty based on Freetown on the West African coast. The big AMC escorted convoys from here to the English Channel and then returned again to Freetown without putting into a British port. These exacting and uncomfortable duties continued until April 1940, when two events of significance occurred.

The first was that the Admiralty decided to switch the *Jervis Bay* to the North Atlantic, escorting the convoys out of Halifax, Nova Scotia. And the other was the appointment to command of the *Jervis Bay* of Captain Edward Stephen Fogarty Fegen, Royal Navy.

Fegen was a regular officer who had entered Osborne as a cadet in 1904. He was a bachelor of forty-eight, who seldom spoke of his private affairs.

He was a big man, with the classical, fierce look of the aggressive sea captain. His face was craggy and his eyebrows were tufted.

He seemed actually to have been designed for the role, beloved by the British, of leading a large company of men to flaming death, against impossible, overwhelming odds. And, at the end of 1940, that's exactly what he did.

What made it even better for the British public was that Fegen appeared to save thirty-two ships out of the thirty-seven in his convoy when he died.

But he didn't save my brother Mart's ship that day.

And if it had not been for the stupidity of the German who attacked him, Fogarty Fegen wouldn't have saved many other ships in the convoy either.

11
ON THE DOLE

The years 1936 to 1939 are not years that I care to recall as far as my own progress is concerned. I hated like hell to be different to the other kids in the street and yet at first I found myself following a different path to them, without seemingly being able to do anything about it.

Most of my mates left school at fourteen and went to work in factories or the shipyard. By rashly sitting an exam, I found myself going to the Tech day school well after I was fourteen. Luckily, the only subjects for which I turned out to have any sort of flair were English, French and maths. The Tech provided tuition in many more subjects than these and by failing in practically all of the other stupid subjects like woodwork, metalwork and commerce, I managed to pull my average down sufficiently far to fail the whole course and escape school when I was fifteen.

This was particularly disappointing for Mart, who had hoped to see me rise to great things one day, but he took the news philosophically enough, when I told him in the fo'c's'le of the *Dunaff Head*.

'Maybe I can get away to sea now,' I suggested hopefully, but Mart shook his head. 'No chance of that,' he said. 'The old lady would pull me limb from limb if I suggested any such thing. She wants you to get a collar and tie job.'

'What about my going in the Head Line as an apprentice, on deck?' I asked, but this only drew another negative. 'It costs fifty quid to become an apprentice, and that's before you even buy your gear,' Mart said. 'Who's got that sort of dough?'

'I could sign on as a deck boy, and work for my ticket,' was my final gambit, and for a while Mart looked at me speculatively. 'You could too,' he said, 'but I wouldn't like to see you living like this, even for the few years before getting your ticket,' and he waved his hand and looked around the fo'c's'le.

We were sitting at the mess table. Fragments of the last meal were scattered about. A seven-pound tin of jam sat in the middle of the table near a hard-boiled egg, out of which one spoonful had been scooped. Several slices of rough wheaten bread baked by Danny, the *Dunaff Head*'s diminutive cook, lay about the table. An enamel plate held the remains of what looked like bully-beef hash.

The fo'c's'le could have done with a lick of paint but this, when added, could not have kept this place fresh-looking. The light was poor, provided only by portholes and naked electric light bulbs, and the place smelt strongly of engine oil, Lifebuoy soap and timber from the deck cargo.

'What's the matter with this?' I asked Mart incredulously. I loved it. I would have given ten years of my life to move in beside Mart, to one of the uncomfortable bunks fastened to the bare, dripping plates. To eat preserved eggs that were blue-white inside, and to smear Danny the cook's bread with jam. God, if I could only have told him that I cried in private when he sailed away.

Father aboard the *Dunaff Head* in 1930

Uncle James

Mother

Aunt Berry with Chattie

Tommy (left), Tiny and me

Mart at seventeen

Captain Fogarty Fegen and the *Jervis Bay*

Captain Thomas
Frederick Milner
and the *Kenbane Head*

The *Admiral Scheer*

Me during my RAF years
Below: with pilot Johnny Bates
(right) on a North African
airfield in 1944

But clearly it was no use my thinking about living in the fo'c's'le of a Head Line boat, that was for sure. I was put to work in the end in a warehouse, learning the wholesale drapery trade. A collar and tie job.

It nearly put me crackers. The place was run by a brother and sister, both middle-aged and unmarried. They honestly thought it was a good job, at ten bob a week.

My mate Tommy Walsh, an apprentice shipwright in the shipyard, was earning thirty to thirty-five bob a week without any bother, and getting lovely and dirty at the same time.

I did everything I could to get out of that place. I hated even to mention it to my mates in the evenings, at Canning Street corner, although they all seemed to regard me with respect, because I didn't start until 9.30 a.m. and finished at 5.00 p.m.

At this time the first signs of a temper which was to get me into all sorts of trouble later on in life began to appear. When I was sixteen and a bit, and had been about a year in the job, I cheeked the boss directly for the first time, after taking a tonguing for some trivial offence.

'Don't you try that York Street stuff on me,' the boss said. He was tall, thin, and had a prominent, bobbing Adam's apple. His more forceful sister dominated him entirely. 'Just watch yourself,' he said, trembling a little.

'Ah balls!' I rapped back, and walked out of the place, slamming the door violently behind me.

I had taken only a couple of steps down the narrow corridor outside the door, when the sound of crashing glass stopped me dead in my tracks.

I looked over my shoulder warily. The glass which had

formed the entire top half of the door had shattered and slid to the ground. On the other side the boss stood looking at me in pop-eyed horror. His Adam's apple was working violently, and his face was chalk-white with anger and fright. 'You … you're sacked …' he got out eventually. Muttering devout thanks to the Lord, I got out of the place like a scalded cat.

But I hadn't bargained for Mother. The very next day I was back in the warehouse. 'You very nearly lost your job,' said the boss's sister. 'It's a good thing your mother explained about your bad nerves.'

If Chamberlain had only consulted my mother in time, she could have stopped the Second World War from breaking out!

I was seventeen before I got out of that accursed job. Even then I had to resign and tell Mother a pack of lies about business being bad and staff being cut. One difficulty that arose out of this deception, however, was that my dole was stopped for six weeks because I had left work voluntarily. I had the devil of a job to prevent Mother from representing me at the tribunal.

I must say I had a most enjoyable time of it on the dole, mainly because I was at last the same as the other lads in the street. The day's programme usually began at about half past eight, when I would start helping Mother about the house. Then about eleven o'clock one of my unemployed mates would call and we would more than likely go for a stroll around the docks. If we ran into Uncle Thomas we were likely to touch for a couple of bob, usually delivered together with a lecture chiding me for being idle.

'It's all right for a ballicks like him,' Uncle Thomas would say, pointing to whoever I was with – someone totally unknown to him, I might add – 'but you've got brains. You should be in a good job instead of arsing around here.' I had more trouble than enough in pacifying my mates after such incidents. It generally took me a long time to persuade them that Uncle Thomas insulted nearly everybody he met, including me, when he felt like it.

There was a powerful contrast between my uncles in their behaviour, I must say. Thomas was as rough as they come. But Uncle James – he overdramatised everything. Once, with the whites of his eyes showing, he related to me his reaction to a soldier who had made some sort of disparaging remark to him. James was working in some kind of capacity in Sandes' Soldiers' Home in Clifton Street, at the time.

'I said to this merchant "Who in the name of the just Jasus do you think you're talkin' till, ye ignorant-lookin' gulpin ye?" and he lucked at me for a minnit an' he says, "Oi doant want enny trouble Paddy" – he was English, wouldn't ye know it? So I says to him, "I've a frigging good mind to take that cow's bladder of a face o' yours and bounce it round and round them four walls."'

'Why? What did he do to you?' I asked him.

'I suppose he blinked his eyes rather loudly,' said our Jim, who was a great cynic, but it turned out in this case that the Englishman had snapped his fingers at Uncle James, as well as saying something nasty, and I must admit it would have set me off too.

Uncle Sammy on the other hand, was the original straight-faced comic. He was superb at it.

He had been married young, to a marvellously loveable

woman, Aunt Sarah, who was a great favourite of ours. And the kids had arrived regularly every eighteen months or so, in this very happy union.

At funerals and weddings and other gatherings of the family Uncle Sammy loved to refer to his lack of stature in this connection. He had a round innocent face, and he would make an O with his mouth to make himself even more angelic. Then he would tell the story of the big woman next door to him, who had no family.

'When I'm going out to work in the morning,' he would say, in a prim, shy voice, 'this big woman always manages to be out, scrubbing the step. I can see her looking at me, and wondering at me, so small, and yet having such a big family.'

'I can tell what she's thinking,' he would say, biting his lip and looking heavenwards. 'She's thinking "How can such a wee man manage it and that big ox of mine can't".'

'I'm sure and certain I saw a tear rolling down that woman's face when I went past her this morning,' he would say, 'I thought by the way she was looking at me that she was going to throw the floor cloth over me and catch me for her own purposes!' And Uncle Sammy would make a little steeple with his fingers and swing his legs on the chair, whilst those around him roared, and Mother shushed him, scandalised, but laughing all the same.

Another way for us to pass away the idle hours in those days was in the bookies. I must say I never stood the slightest chance of getting caught up in the racing game – even though Mart was a pretty hefty punter when he was at home – but it wasn't a bad way to get through an hour or two. It only took three of us to put up twopence each and we were in business with a tanner double.

By this time my brother Jim had joined us on the dole, and he and I were great observers of the passing scene. We derived great amusement from some of the characters who frequented the bookies. Many of the old-timers who couldn't afford spectacles used to hold the glass from an electric torch to magnify the racing sheets. Our Jim could imitate their posture and screwed up facial expressions to the life. Pretending to smoke an old short-stemmed pipe, Jim used to hold his cupped hand to his mouth, suck air in, and then go: 'Pism. Pism. Pism.'

And that's just the sound the old pipe-smoking punters made, standing studying the horses: 'Pism. Pism. Pism.'

Then there was the pronunciation of the horses' names. If there was a wrong way to put them the punters would find it. One day in the Gibraltar Bar in York Street two hard punters were standing, studying their pints. The bar was empty, but for themselves, and a barman, who was studying himself in the mirror and fancying himself as Clark Gable.

The two o'clock race at Sandown had just been announced off, but the punters had committed themselves ten minutes earlier. One of them had put one pound and the other fifteen shillings on the good thing – a two-year-old called Blanc Mange which, on form, looked as though it could win the race whilst reading the *Belfast News Letter* at the same time.

One punter looked at the clock – three minutes past two. He picked up his pint, took an absent-minded swig out of it and put the glass down. The other punter studied a decorative mahogany barrel-end. He had seen this barrel-end a thousand times before, but now looked at it intently, as though it was a newly-found sarcophagus, raised from the tomb of Tut ...

Suddenly the door burst open and the silence was shattered. A newcomer entered the bar. He was sharp-looking, thin, and had a prematurely aged face for a chap of twenty-one or so. This man had punter written all over him.

The two men already at the bar looked at him in silence. They hadn't the courage to speak, to ask whether their horse, Blanc Mange, had won.

'Blanc Mange won that race,' said the third man. As one, the pair of gamblers at the bar swore, tore their dockets up and flung them to the floor.

'Didn't back it?' asked their informant sympathetically.

'Never even heard of it, never mind back it,' said one punter miserably.

'Never heard of it? Sure it was the favourite!' cried the other in disbelief.

'Blawmong? Favourite? No it isn't,' they said. 'Our horse Blancey Manchey was the favourite.'

A minute later the curtain comes down on two happy punters scrabbling on the floor of the Gibraltar Bar for the constituent parts of their winning dockets.

And that story's true. At least our Jim told me it was, when we were on the dole together in 1938.

12
PRELUDE TO THE SLAUGHTER II
THE *ADMIRAL SCHEER*

It requires something of an effort for a citizen of the United Kingdom to appreciate fully the fact that the sailors in Hitler's navy were actually proud of their service and considered it to have a fine tradition.

When you think of the British at war in 1939 you think immediately of the fleets of warships of all classes deployed in the Far and Middle East and in home waters; of the island under siege and of the daring and skilful seamen who carried defence into attack time and time again to send the invader reeling. This is what tradition is all about, wouldn't you imagine?

If so, then how on earth could Germans serving in a puny little fleet – a withered, deformed stump of an arm attached to a huge body – possibly feel pride and fervour in time of national danger? Hitler's surface fleet was locked in harbours that were watched closely by Coastal Command of the RAF. If a major unit of the German Navy did make the attempt to break out into the sea-lanes it faced discovery by patrolling light forces and probably annihilation by the British dreadnoughts that were on permanent short stand by.

Where was the glory in such a life? For heaven's sake, they ran at the first sight of opposition, didn't they? What sort of sportsmanship would you call that?

Yet you can be sure that the Germans who served in the navy loved their service deeply. They showed their pride openly, to an extent unknown in the British Navy. And their values were totally different from those of the British.

Given an understanding of the difference in values held by the sailors of both navies, it follows that the Germans should see actions such as, for example, the *Rawalpindi*'s sinking as triumphs.

With this armed merchant cruiser's destruction the German surface fleet had been blooded. The *Rawalpindi* was, after all, a warship, and it had been sunk. And the whole home fleet had not been able to stop it.

It's the last reason that was the important one. The Germans in Hitler's navy were taking on Goliath in the British Navy. The only sensible way to go about this was to go for the jugular vein – attack the merchant fleet that the mighty British Navy was supposed to protect and the U-boats were intended to handle that aspect of the war. The role of the surface battle fleet was to draw off the heavy surface forces of the British from areas where the Germans were sensitive. The German Admiralty tacticians were past masters at this: the very fact that a big enemy naval unit was anchored in a certain harbour meant that major British forces had to be kept in readiness to deal with a possible breakout.

The crews of the battle cruisers and battleships accepted their role whilst in harbour, but it was only natural that they should itch for the breakout.

Easily the most successful breakout of the war as far as the Germans were concerned was the voyage in 1940 of the battleship *Scheer* from 27 October 1940 to 1 April 1941, but before this the Germans had sent a good many armed merchant cruisers of their own into the Allies' sea-lanes.

These disguised raiders were at sea throughout the whole of 1940. In general they were smaller than the British AMCs, and slower, but they were much better armed and far better managed.

Capable of long cruising performance, the German raiders went in for a variety of devices to deceive their enemy. Telescopic topmasts, dummy funnels, dummy deck houses, false deck cargoes and frequent repainting at sea were all employed in order to keep the British guessing.

Usually they were armed with six to eight modern 5.9-inch guns, torpedo tubes and even in some cases spotter aircraft. They were provided with their own fleet of supply ships, of which *Nordmark* and *Altmark* were the most notable.

The first merchant raider to leave Germany was the *Atlantis*, in March 1940. The *Orion* sailed in April. The *Wedder* went marauding in May, the *Thor* and *Pinguin* in June, and the *Komet* left Bergen in July. Thus, by the middle of 1940, six well-armed German raiders were at sea.

Working together, *Orion* and *Komet* sank the *Rangitane*, a 16,500-ton liner, after she had left Auckland, New Zealand. The *Orion* laid mines off Auckland, and one of these mines sank the British vessel *Niagara*, carrying £2.5 million in gold ingots.

The *Thor* had sunk six Allied merchant ships when she met the British armed merchant cruiser *Alcantara* on

28 July 1940. In the fight which followed the *Thor* had the better of her bigger opponent. The *Alcantara* suffered serious damage in this encounter, but *Thor*, too, received extensive damage.

On 5 December 1940 the *Thor* ran across another British AMC, the *Caernarvon Castle*, off the east coast of South America. Once again a big, poorly-armed British ship was pummelled whilst *Thor* escaped without damage.

After this the British cruisers *Enterprise*, *Cumberland* and *Newcastle* were sent out to hunt for *Thor*, but she escaped.

Pinguin, another of the German raiders, sank and captured twenty-five Allied ships, totalling over one hundred thousand tons, including three large Norwegian whale factory ships. Four hundred merchant marine prisoners taken by *Pinguin* were safely taken to France on board the captured ship *Storstad*.

Atlantis, the first of the raiders to sail from the homeland, actually established the pattern for future breakouts, and her route through the Denmark Strait became the standard route for all commerce raiders in Hitler's navy.

Between them these disguised raiders throughout their careers sank or captured eighty-two ships, amounting to nearly a quarter of a million tons. In fact, most of the three hundred thousand tons of merchant shipping that fell victim to German surface ships in the last three months of 1940 were accounted for by the splendidly equipped and excellently manned armed merchant raiders.

It is of interest to the naval historian to note that the British Navy laid all its emphasis on hunting the surface raider, and hardly any priority was given to tracking down the ships that supplied these wolves of the sea-lanes.

So methodical was the German Command that in 1937 they laid down four ships which were to have no other function than that of supplying raiders at sea in time of war. They were the *Altmark, Nordmark, Dithmarschen* and *Ermland.* These vessels, which were, in fact, warships themselves, were like tankers in appearance and fully loaded they displaced 22,500 tons. They were 580 feet long, had a 70-foot beam and drew 30 feet at the maximum. They were capable of 21 knots.

Each ship could carry more than 10,000 tons of fuel oil and 300 tons of lubricant. There were special petrol storage tanks for use by the raiders' aircraft and there were storerooms for spare parts, clothing and munitions.

Heavy ammunition was carried for battleships like the *Deutschland* and *Scheer* and a plentiful supply of torpedoes was carried both for surface ships and U-boats. The supply ships were armed with two 20mm anti-aircraft guns and three 150mm guns, plus several machine guns. Unlike the Royal Navy, the Germans manned their supply ships with naval ratings.

In August 1939 the pocket battleships *Graf Spee* and *Deutschland* sailed to pre-arranged sea positions. The *Altmark* also sailed in order to supply the *Graf Spee*, and *Nordmark* put to sea in support of the *Deutschland*. By 15 November *Deutschland* had completed her sortie and was back in Gotenhafen; she had met and drawn supplies from the *Nordmark* four times during the voyage. The paltry 'catch' of the *Deutschland* in this foray amounted to the British ship *Stonegate*, sunk six hundred miles east of Bermuda, the US vessel *City of Flint*, which was captured and subsequently became the subject of angry protests from neutral USA before being set free again, and the small freighter *Lorentz W Henson*, a Norwegian-owned ship of less than two thousand tons.

The *Graf Spee* never returned from her breakout. Her end is detailed in a later chapter, but she met and was supplied by *Altmark* no less than five times during her three-month voyage.

In a celebrated action carried out in Norwegian waters, on 16 February 1940, Captain Vian of the British destroyer *Cossack* sent a boarding party on to the *Altmark*, released 299 merchant navy prisoners from 9 ships which the *Graf Spee* had sunk, and brought them back to Leith for a most unexpected reunion later with their wives and families.

Later, when *Nordmark* set course from Gotenhafen on 17 October 1940 on her second voyage, the curtain was just going up on the most celebrated breakout drama of all, from the German point of view. This voyage was made by the *Admiral Scheer* – a ship that gave the British Navy the biggest fright it had had since Dunkirk.

This particular raider *did* come back to Germany after its breakout, on 27 October 1940, and by the time she dropped anchor in Kiel on April Fools' Day 1941, she had added almost one hundred thousand tons to the appalling toll of British merchant shipping lost at this black period of the war.

The Germans never used the term pocket battleship. To them the *Scheer* was a heavy cruiser, or a battle cruiser. She was launched at Wilhelmshaven in 1933, the year Hitler became Chancellor of Germany, and named after the man who commanded the German naval forces at the Battle of Skagerrak, or, as the British say, Jutland. Her sister-ships were the *Graf Spee* and *Deutschland*, later to be renamed *Lutzow*.

The *Scheer's* operational range was nineteen thousand miles. At the start of the war her silhouette was changed when the fighting mast which identified her at a great distance was taken away. After this the *Scheer's* appearance was similar to that of the *Scharnhorst* or *Gneisenau*.

In peacetime her complement was 1,100; another 100 men were added in wartime. She was a ship of 10,000 tons, with a top speed of almost 28 knots. Her two great turrets were each fitted with three 11-inch guns. As well as this her secondary armament consisted of eight 5.9-inch guns, and there was also a plentiful spread of 20mm and machine guns for anti-aircraft cover.

A most important addition to the *Scheer's* fighting equipment was an Arada 196 floatplane which carried a pilot and an observer/gunner.

But far and away her most vital weapon was one that will surprise many British, brought up to believe that the Allies had always led the world in the use of effective radar. The *Scheer*, at the end of 1940, carried a radar installation that was well in advance of anything used by British warships and indeed it was well into 1941 before the British Navy got on terms with their enemy in sea-borne radar equipment.

During her historic voyage in 1940-41 the *Scheer* was commanded by Captain Theodor Krancke, a former OC (officer commanding) of the Naval Academy, and the man who was put in charge of operational preparations for the campaign at sea against Norway in the spring of 1940.

Just three days before war broke out in 1939 Adolf Hitler

issued his instructions to the German Naval Command: 'The Navy will concentrate on commerce destruction directed, especially against England.'

Captain Theodor Krancke and the *Admiral Scheer* certainly played their parts in implementing that directive. Krancke did it so well that every man in his crew got the Iron Cross – a unique honour. He claimed to have sunk 151,000 tons on his voyage; actually the figure was 99,059 tons.

Krancke destroyed 17 ships. One of them was the AMC *Jervis Bay*.

And another was the *Kenbane Head*.

Mart's ship.

13
DOING OUR BIT

Tommy went off and joined the North Irish Horse in September 1939 and went to Portrush with the regiment. I went down to the Royal Navy and joined up as a seaman in October, and got ready to sail away any day. But for some reason which baffles me till this day I heard no more from the Navy. By January 1940 my pals were beginning to look at me a bit oddly, so, having heard from John Young, a good mate of mine, that the RAF were whipping recruits away in next to no time, down to them I went, and never mentioned anything about my application with the Navy.

The question then arose, of course, as to what trade or profession I was to follow in the RAF. I was unconcerned. I knew absolutely nothing about aeroplanes, although I had been working as a riveter in Short and Harland's aircraft factory for some months beforehand, until my natural ineptitude with tools got me the sack.

'Riveter, were you?' the RAF Sergeant said. 'Righto – you'll be a flight rigger.' And that's what I became. A flight rigger.

A funny thing happened in John Young's case. Old John was a tiler by trade, by which is meant fitting tiles on floors, pavements, fireplaces and anywhere else tiles are supposed to go.

'Wot's your tryde,' asked the cockney clerk in the recruiting office.

'Tiler,' said John.

The clerk filled in forms accordingly.

It was only when John was in Padgate, Lancs, undergoing his documentation that he discovered the RAF were about to put him to work in the tailor's shop! I don't know what trade John actually chose to follow at that crisis in his affairs but I know he was too hard in the neck to fancy working in a tailor's shop. In fact he ended up as a very proficient air gunner, but that was years later.

One good thing about the long wait to go away was that I took a good close look at the family for the first time in my life. The casualty lists appearing in the papers – nearly all merchant navy and Royal Navy personnel in that early stage of the war – helped to point up the fact that I was not going off on any Church Lads' Brigade camp this time.

I became very close to Chattie, our only sister. Chattie was very much taken for granted in our family because she had not developed a strong personality of her own. Nor did she show any positive indication of gallivanting around after the boys, although she was a good-looking girl.

Six years older than I was, Chattie had been brought up too close to the church way of life to gravitate easily to the dance halls, where she might have met a boy she liked. Although she puffed the odd cigarette and took an occasional sherry, she was innocent and totally without sophistication all her life.

Chattie was about five foot four. Her hair was brown and

her complexion was beautifully pink and white. When she was younger she had been quite plump but from her early twenties on she had a very attractive figure. She had teeth like Mart – beautifully white and even.

Her eyes were brown and her brown eyes were nearly always turned on her brothers when she was at home. For Chattie lived a quiet life – three times a week she went out, usually to the pictures, with a quiet girlfriend – and we boys were the ones who had the excitement. Chattie loved to hear about all our adventures and we could always be sure that when we were telling the tale in the house, Chattie's soft eyes would be fixed on us: she would be storing up every scrap of information to be told later on to her chum Margaret.

There was a hint of romance in Chattie's life once. She sat in the parlour with someone for a bit, but it didn't come to anything. Probably because she didn't know how to make it come to anything, God bless her.

Then, in this period in the last quarter of 1939, there was Mother's sister Aunt Berry. She had moved house along with Uncle James when he had to leave Mackey Street a few years earlier, but surprisingly James had decided to give up the bachelor's life in 1939, and settle down with a lively, dark-eyed girl called Molly.

This meant that Aunt Berry, whose name was really Beryl, moved into her own place, or, to put it more accurately, it meant that she established a headquarters for herself up the Oldpark Road and went to live with her brothers and sisters as the notion took her.

I'd better go into detail here about Aunt Berry. Particularly about her leg …

Our family used to regard Aunt Berry's leg as part of the furniture and fittings.

We were fascinated by it sometimes, mind you, but only when she took it off. When I was exploring her house as a wee boy I would sometimes see through the partly open door of her bedroom, Aunt Berry's leg propped up against the dressing table, silk stocking and shoe still attached.

It never failed to stop me dead, but I would never hang about staring at it, or anything like that. One thing none of us did, or our cousins either, was to even mention it to each other. We didn't just think enough of it, and anyway it was her business not ours.

As far as the neighbours and others were concerned it didn't arise as a topic of conversation. The poorer people are the more manners they have about that sort of thing.

In any case Aunt Berry was very well respected in all the districts where the various sprigs of the family lived. She visited us all in turn, and she was well known in all the localities.

She was very ladylike, you see. The limp in her walk was carried off in a very refined sort of way. Indeed I always think it added to her stylish look when she was out on the street, and I might as well tell you that, being so impressionable about these things, I tried limping a bit myself, I admired it so much in Aunt Berry. All that happened in my case, however, was that Mother made me put my right foot with the shoe still on it into a basin of warm water. She thought my shoe was pinching, and that was an old dodge to fix it.

Before I leave that talk I might as well tell you that there was a boy called Stevie somebody who lived near us in

Tiger's Bay when I was a youngster and Stevie was always pulling at the crotch of his trousers. Actually they were too small for him but I didn't know that then. I thought it was a mannerism, and a very interesting one at that, so I started doing it too, till Jack gave me a boot in the backside and told me to stop continually scratching at myself in such a part of my body.

But back to Aunt Berry's leg. I remember one time when somebody outside the family stared – really stared, I mean – at her leg. My playmate Billy Henry did once, when his mother was visiting our house, and Billy had been put in a corner of the tiny kitchen in Cosgrave Street to play with my brothers and myself, whilst Aunt Berry, in her elegant way, engaged Mrs Henry in conversation.

We were showing Billy our few toys and gewgaws, not that they amounted to very much, dear knows, and we happened to turn up an old set of feathered darts.

Billy and I started to throw the darts into the worn linoleum near the chairs where the women were seated and I overdid things as usual and threw a dart clean into Aunt Berry's leg.

What fractured Billy Henry's composure, really, was the fact that Aunt Berry obviously didn't know about the dart. She sat smiling and talking and gesturing in her genteel way, with this dart dug right into her leg. In the middle of the shin it was, actually.

Before I could bring Billy Henry back to this world I had to give him a proper dunt. He sat there, riveted, with eyes like banjos.

He was hypnotised, watching Aunt Berry, with her graceful arm and hand movements, describing one of her impossibly detailed dreams to Mrs Henry. 'I was in a garden, Minnie,' she was saying, 'all surrounded by the most beeeaut-iful white blossoms, and there, coming towards me, with like a morning suit and a top hat on, was this beeeaut-iful looking man.' Billy couldn't budge. His mouth had fallen open. He kept staring at the dart.

I had to give him a second shove and carry through, sort of, falling against Aunt Berry's knee and smartly slipping the dart out of her leg without letting her down.

For the rest of Billy Henry's stay in our house he kept throwing sideways glances at Aunt Berry's leg, and frowning slightly, in bewilderment. I suppose he knew better than to say anything. Otherwise he'd have collected a dig in the gub.

Although there wasn't a big lot of extra space in our house, with six of us living there, it was still taken for granted that room would be made for Aunt Berry when our turn came round for her visit.

When she left after one of these visits, the house was in somewhat of a state of uproar. Always for the one reason. No matter whose home she stayed in, she picked out one member of the family to pamper and spoil, and the others, of course, objected strongly. So did the parents, but it made no difference to Aunt Berry.

All the same, I always thought she was pretty stylish. She was in her forties when I was a boy at school, but I remember her as a really lovely woman. She had a long, graceful neck and dark hair in soft waves. There was a way she had of holding her head back and tilted a bit that was really striking. Like a model.

Aunt Berry was medium sized. Her eyes were soft and

grey. Dreaming eyes. Even in my boyhood I made allowance for her habit of making a fuss of just one kid in each family. I knew that she was troubled a bit; her dreaming eyes showed it, and the long detailed stories of her dreams that she told.

She carried a bit of a tale, too, from one house to the other, but nothing that Aunt Berry did could draw anything except mild exasperation from her brothers and sisters. She couldn't really upset them. My mother and all the others of Aunt Berry's family knew that, by buying extra clothes and sweets and toys for one special youngster in each house, Aunt Berry was making a substitute for the loved one that could never share her own life.

When she was only twelve, a beautiful tomboy, Aunt Berry thought nothing of the blister that formed on her heel. But there was no penicillin in those days to counter septic poisoning ...

After they took her leg off and gave her a crutch the doctors told her family to send her away to the country for recuperation.

It must have drawn a wry smile to her parents' faces. Some hopes! What the family did was to send Berry's brothers out to take her in their care to the sooty grasses and half-strangled shrubs of Alexandra Park on the Antrim Road. Here, with either Thomas, James, Hugh or Billy (who was blown to pieces in the First War), she sat on a park bench when the weather allowed it, watching others walk and run and laugh and enjoy themselves. Watching young girls go by on the arms of young men. Berry was lovelier than any of them, but it was the others who were walking towards whatever happiness that life held.

So Aunt Berry would have had to do a terrible lot more than she did before the patience of her brothers and sisters and nephews and nieces wore out. As for me – I always thought she was a knockout.

Aunt Berry always had plenty of style. Any amount of it. And nowadays style is just about the rarest commodity there is.

The last major event to happen before 1940 in our family occurred when Dad called Mart into his cabin on board the *Dunaff Head* one night in late October 1939. They were within sight of the Irish coast, homeward bound.

'It wouldn't be fair on your mother if the two of us stayed on the one ship, Mart,' he said. 'I've been through one war. It's going to get rough. If we were both lost it would finish her.' Mart of course agreed.

'I can't ask you to move ship,' Mart said. 'You're nicely fixed up here. I'll pay off and wait for the next Head boat.'

So it was agreed. Dad was fifty-seven at the time. Mart was twenty-five. It never entered either of their heads to stay ashore until the war was over. This was because they were seamen. You might as well ask a grocer to trim the bunkers as ask seamen to work ashore.

'By the way,' Dad asked, as Mart got up to leave his cabin, 'what's the next Head boat due to pay off?'

'The *Kenbane*,' Mart said.

14

PRELUDE TO THE SLAUGHTER III
THE *KENBANE HEAD*

There is a place almost at the very top of Ireland that looks directly out on Rathlin Island and across the pent-up waters of the North Channel to Kintyre and beyond.

This is Kenbane Head, the 'White Head', five miles to the west of the great blue anvil of Fair Head.

Here, the year round, the wind creams the offshore waters and rushes up the cliff face, to break on the old battlements and weathered walls of Kenbane Castle. Only the ravens live there now, with the seabirds for visitors.

Kenbane Castle was built over four hundred years ago by Colla MacDonnell, Captain of the Route. Colla was appointed by his brother James, who was head of the Islay MacDonnells and Lord of the Isles, in succession to Donald Dubh. Another brother was one of the greatest warriors in all Ireland, Sorley Boy MacDonnell, he of the two-handed sword and the yellow hair, streaming in the wind.

Colla, dark, fearless, and a noted horseman, lost Kenbane Castle for a short time to the forces of the Englishman Sir Thomas Cusack, in 1551, but it was quickly regained, and

Colla lived there without further interruption until his death in 1558.

The English, sailing to punish the Scots on Rathlin, marked this headland on the northern sea passage from Carrickfergus. The Elizabethans knew that, if they sailed to the landward of the rock that is called Carrickavaan, three cables out from Kenbane Head, they were lost, either on the reef, or in the eddy.

The MacDonnells knew this coast well, it goes without saying – they sailed the dark and turbulent waters between Dalriada and Scotland as naturally as they rode their half-wild horses on the springy turf ashore.

Colla MacDonnell, a warrior and a sailor, would have approved the naming of a ship after Kenbane Head. This ship, born in 1919, 361 years after Colla's death, replaced another lost in a war. She herself was to die in battle, but her resting place is a long, long way from the green and purple coast of North Ireland, and the white headland after which she was named.

When the *Kenbane Head* was five years old, one of her firemen was Marriott McAughtry, then forty-two. He did one trip only in this ship, a voyage sandwiched between a six-month trip to New Zealand and back on the *Port Wellington*, and a return to the familiar comfort of the tiny cabin in the *Dunaff Head*. Master of the ship on this trip in 1924 was Captain McFerran.

Captain Erele Black, retired commodore of the Head Line, and one-time ordinary seaman in the line, sailed as a brand-new third officer in the *Kenbane Head* in 1920. He recalls her as a ship that handled well and had no bad habits.

Built by Workman Clark in 1919, she had a straight stem and a counter stern. The old salts used to say that ships like this were built by the mile and chopped off in lengths as required. In fact the Head Line's deep-sea ships were custom-built for the Western Ocean run.

But for her long fo'c's'le head she would have been a three-islander. She carried deck cargo on the bridge deck and poop. There were four holds. The deep tank carried water ballast on the way out and cargo coming home.

The *Kenbane Head* had a split superstructure, with the bridge house separate from the funnel and engine casing. The triple expansion engine gave an average speed of nine knots on twenty-five tons coal consumption. For an extra two knots, another eight tons was added to the coal consumption.

The deck and engine-room crews' accommodation was in the fo'c's'le. The entrance on the fo'c's'le head was covered against the head seas by a curved scuttleway. There were no hot water facilities in the fo'c's'le. If the weather was too bad for hot water to be carried by the crew from the galley, then they washed in cold water.

Six firemen, three trimmers and three greasers were accommodated in the port side fo'c's'le of the *Kenbane Head*. Their sleeping quarters were crude, to say the least, consisting of steel bunks fastened to sweating steel plates that were without effective insulation. There was no individual privacy in the crews' quarters.

Once a week the master inspected the fo'c's'le, with the mate, the chief engineer and the chief steward. In those days masters were not interested in the standard of crew accommodation provided by the company, merely in its cleanliness. It seems almost beyond belief that first-trippers who sailed in ships like the *Kenbane Head* had to be 'spoken for', as though it was some sort of privilege. And this even as comparatively recently as the 1940s.

An examination of the Line's expansion programme since its inception in 1877 will give some idea of the profits the company must have been making. Between 1879 and 1900, fifteen ships were built, as the potential of the trade became apparent. Five more were added before the outbreak of the First World War, and ten more were added to the fleet between the wars, although these replaced ships sunk by the Germans.

But despite the fact that the trade was making profits, the crews had roughly the same accommodation throughout the whole building programme. Some might say it was not much better than the facilities afforded to the Irish immigrants in the bowels of nineteenth-century sailing ships going to the New World over the same route that the Head Line ships followed.

By late 1940 the *Kenbane Head* was an elderly lady of twenty-one. She was under the command of Captain Thomas Frederick Milner, an elderly gentleman of sixty-five by then.

Captain Milner was a low-set man, inclined to be brusque and quick-tempered. He had no hobbies. Born in 1875, Milner did not come from a family with a seafaring tradition, yet both he and his brother became ships' masters.

He served his apprenticeship in one of Tedford of

Belfast's sailing ships, the *Bluebell*, and took his certificate in sail. During the First World War he was an officer in the Royal Naval Reserve, with the rank of Lieutenant Commander. Before taking command of the *Kenbane Head* he had been master of the *Fanad Head* and *Dunaff Head*. Milner was a competent and reliable sailor, of the old school.

When the *Kenbane Head* under Milner signed on a crew on 11 September 1940 for a voyage to Dublin, Fowey, Three Rivers, Montreal, Halifax, Nova Scotia, and Belfast, the company had no trouble in getting a crew despite the horrifying losses at the time. Here is the total ship's complement for her final trip:

			AGE
Master	T.F. Milner	Islandmagee	65
Chief Officer	W. French	Birmingham	40
2nd Officer	G. Leckey	Holywood	27
3rd Officer	W. Bell	Belfast	26
Chief Engineer	W.J. McIlroy	Dundrum	59
2nd Engineer	H. Carson	Belfast	46
3rd Engineer	T. Smith	Belfast	24
4th Engineer	D. Wilson	Belfast	23
1st Radio Officer	P. Cahill	Cork	37
2nd Radio Officer	L. Graves	Birkenhead	33
Apprentices	G. Crangle	Belfast	21
	N. Walsh	Limerick	17
	R. Green	Kilkeel	18
Bosun	W. Wright	Belfast	43
Lamptrimmer	D. Donovan	Clonakilty	33

ABs	J. McQuillan	Glenravel	25
	S. Boyd	Ballyhalbert	20
	F. Miller	Ballyhalbert	19
	D. McKay	Belfast	24
Sailors	W. McBride	Belfast	20
	D. Fullerton	Ballyhalbert	21
	D. Allister	Belfast	20
	D. Pritchard	Ballyhalbert	21
Donkeyman	J. McGuigan	Belfast	42
Storekeeper	J. Laidlaw	Edinburgh	64
Greaser	A. McDonald	Belfast	54
Firemen/Trimmers	J. Swain	Dunmurry	41
	J. McMichael	Belfast	37
	J. Barry	Carrickfergus	29
	B. Henry	Belfast	39
	J. Emerson	Belfast	20
	J.L. McGuigan	Belfast	47
	H. Shaw	Carrickfergus	33
	D. Davies	Port Talbot	45
	M. McAughtry	Belfast	27
Chief Steward	J. Dickey	Belfast	34
2nd Steward	F. McCaw	Belfast	28
Assistant Steward	R. Primmer	Portsmouth	19
Chief Cook	G. Heatley	Belfast	37
2nd Cook	R.J. Moore	Carrickfergus	19
Assistant Cook	H. Bloor	Canada	18
Gunner	R. Drinkwater	Birmingham	27
Carpenter	J. Belshaw	Ballywalter	36

Leslie Graves, the second radio officer, and Reggie Primmer, an assistant steward, were first-trippers.

McQuillan, an able seaman (AB), was ex–*Dunaff Head* and McCaw, a second steward, was ex–*Torr Head*.

All the rest of the crew were regulars in the *Kenbane Head* and many had been sailors in her for years. To those readers for whom the term 'average age' has a meaning, then this value for the *Kenbane Head*'s crew – officers and men – was thirty-two. But a more informative study of their ages is by way of the following table:

Under 20	6
20–29	17
30–39	9
40–49	7
50–59	2
60–65	2

Twenty of the crew of the *Kenbane Head* were either thirty years of age or over – almost half of her complement.

Of the forty-three in the crew, forty-one knew all about the risks involved, having sailed the Western Ocean and run the gauntlet already. Yet here they were, on 11 September 1940, signing on again. And doing so in Belfast, where there was work at long last. Good well-paid work; better paid than the Head Line's nine pounds per month. Belfast was unbombed, as yet. There was no conscription. Unlike Britain there was any amount of good food available too.

These civilian seamen combatants were taking chances far greater than those facing any of the uniformed services. And they were doing so by free choice.

Twenty out of forty-three of them were aged thirty or

over. Eleven were forty or over. Take any merchant ship at the time and you had the same picture. That's what finally puts the merchant service ahead of all others in the gallantry stakes.

Signing-on time is a time for kidding and badinage. There is also the occasional reunion of old shipmates long parted. There is an impatience among the seamen at signing-on time. The spell ashore is over. Time to earn some more money.

In September 1940 the leg-pulling was still evident. Seamen who have sailed together have a bond which is not equalled in any other walk of life. The large numbers accommodated in the fo'c's'le of the Head Line ships made this bond even stronger than usual. Crew members were flung together to such an extent that life would have been very difficult indeed if they could not have lived amicably together.

Long years before the formation of ecumenical groups or any other bodies designed to help Catholics understand Protestants or vice versa, the Head Line crews had mastered the whole business without any fuss at all. When they were ashore they visited each other's homes across the working-class religious divide as a matter of routine, and they thought nothing at all of drinking in each other's pubs.

Catholics and Protestants struck up friendships with each other, not for the reason that Ulstermen ashore have done for generations – the attraction of opposites and the novelty of the thing – but because they were good shipmates.

So the old hands of the *Kenbane Head* would have been glad to see each other again after the ten days or so spent ashore. But there was a sober constraint upon them all: the thought of the North Atlantic passage.

They talked about it, with an occasional tightening of the lips and a resigned shrug of the shoulders.

Jimmy Dickey, the chief steward, had been sixteen years at sea. He had been on the *Fanad Head* when she was shelled and sunk by the U–30 on 14 September 1939, almost exactly a year earlier. That 'effort', as Jimmy put it, had involved twelve hours in an overcrowded lifeboat before a destroyer had picked them up. The other *Kenbane Head* crew members listened to Jimmy's views on the war with respect. He told them that he thought it would get worse before it got better.

Billy McBride, one of the sailors, wasn't impressed by the Head Line. He had been to Gravesend sea school when he was sixteen and had sailed since then in more comfortable ships than the Head boats. He had only come back to Belfast to remind himself of what the place of his birth was like.

Jim Emerson, a trimmer, was on his second trip. He was on the *Kenbane Head* because Mart McAughtry had got him the job. Jim had always wanted to go to sea. He was an only child, so his mother had put up very strong resistance to this idea indeed.

But Jim was twenty and had to have his way. His parents thought that the only good thing about the whole arrangement was that Mart had taken Jim under his wing, arranging for them to share the watch.

This certainly suited Jim Emerson. He thought the world

of Mart McAughtry. He wanted to stay in close touch with Mart.

And Jim Emerson did. He certainly did. They both died together, almost at the same moment. Mart and Jim Emerson.

15
PER ARDUA
AD ASTRA

It somehow seems unfair that I should be unable to remember the details of my last days with my brother Mart. But I can't and that's a fact.

It was in January 1940 that the *Kenbane Head* tied up in Pollock Dock, Belfast. Towards the end of January. I remember this because it was about three weeks before I was due to enlist in the RAF, and that was 19 February. I went on board to see him, just like old times.

The fo'c's'le of the *Kenbane Head* was a much gloomier place than that of the *Dunaff Head*. Not only was it less adequately lit, but it looked somehow more in need of freshening up. Indeed the *Kenbane Head* as a ship seemed altogether more run-down that the *Dunaff*, but maybe the *Dunaff* was the same and I hadn't noticed it, because of the place it had had in my affections all my life. It could be that the Head Line ships in general weren't all that smart looking after all, if the truth be told.

Mart, by the time he and I clasped hands in greeting in January 1940, was a man of changed circumstances. He was going strong with Maggie Keel and marriage was only months away for them.

Maggie Keel lived at 84 Hillman Street, exactly seventeen houses below our own house, and in the same block. She seemed naturally to have dropped into Mart's life in the previous year or so. In no time at all it was as if they had always been together.

It wasn't all that surprising really. Not only were the Keels our neighbours but they had been to St Barnabas' public elementary school with us, their boys were in the church organisations with us, and Maggie and Mart had crossed paths goodness knows how many times before they started going out together.

But saving up to get married didn't affect Mart's generous giving-hand and I remember he slipped me ten bob as soon as he was scrubbed and dressed to go ashore.

'Still out of work?' he asked. I nodded happily. Being unemployed had never depressed me. I picked up his sea bag.

'I've got a job for you on the *Kenbane*, if you want it,' he said casually, 'on deck.'

I nearly dropped stone dead right there in the fo'c's'le. 'What?' I almost shouted. He smiled. 'You always wanted to go to sea, didn't you?' he asked.

'But what about Mother?' I wanted to know. 'Haven't you told me a hundred times she didn't want me to go to sea?'

'She wrote to me this trip,' Mart said, as we climbed the fo'c's'le steps together. 'She wasn't happy about the way you enjoy being on the dole.' He looked at me out of the corner of his eye, smiling.

'Hell bloody roast it,' I said angrily. 'I've joined the bloody RAF.'

'Can't you get out of it?' Mart asked. I shook my head miserably.

'I'm pretty sure I can't,' I said. Thinking back on it now, though, I believe that I could have. The real joining-up didn't take place until we were attested in England, but I thought at that time that I was hooked.

The lapses of memory come in now. I recall that the dog-racing was held in the afternoons instead of the evenings because of the blackout regulations and Mart and I went to Celtic Park and called into the Star and Garter afterwards, where Mart had a shandy and I had a mineral.

On another day during that shore break Mart called up and took Uncle Alex – Aunt Lena's husband – out for a few drinks at his local. He was off work sick at the time. This stays in the mind because I had never been in a pub with Uncle Alex before, not being old enough, and I was very curious about the drinking habits of my elders although still teetotal myself.

Mart ordered two bottles of stout for Uncle Alex, a shandy for himself, and a mineral for me. He put the two bottles of stout down in front of Uncle Alex and turned back to the bar for a glass. Before he had even reached the bar counter Uncle Alex picked up a bottle of stout, turned it upside down with the neck in his mouth, and let it run straight down his throat. It was emptied in seconds.

I must have been staring quite openly because, when Uncle Alex put the bottle down again, he smiled at my expression and wiped the back of his hand across his mouth. 'That's the best way to drink stout,' he said, 'branches and all.'

During the hour or so that we were in the bar, Uncle Alex must have sunk a dozen of Guinness easily, half of them with branches and all. When we said goodbye he was still as sober as a judge.

Our talk on the *Kenbane Head*, the outing to Celtic Park and the drinks with Uncle Alex are all that I remember of my last contact with Mart.

I don't even remember bidding him goodbye when he sailed away.

I went across on the Larne–Stranraer steamer on the night of 19 February 1940 to join the RAF. It was a foul night for the crossing. The weather was dreadful.

I had never left Ireland in my life before. Indeed, I had only been away from home for a couple of nights in my life. I sat miserably in the steerage saloon of the Larne–Stranraer steamer. Uncle Alex, who was joining the Pioneer Corps, was going across with me. In the LMS railway station in York Street he had promised Jack that he would look after me as long as we were together, but he had fallen in with a bunch of First War cronies and they were having a smashing time at the bar, putting the Guinness away as hard as they could sink it.

Meanwhile I was so ignorant of the facts of travel at sea that I simply sat in the hot, smoky saloon growing more seasick by the minute. Mother, true to form, had made me polish off a heaped-up plateful of bacon, egg, sausage, tomato and dipped bread just before we left, and this didn't help the argument at all.

Every so often Uncle Alex would break off singing 'Goodbye Dolly Gray' or 'Tipperary' and waltz nimbly across the pitching floor to lean over me. 'You'll be all right,' he would say. 'Go on into the lavatory and bring it up.' And I did. Only God knows how often I did.

I hadn't even the sense to go up on deck and get some fresh air. I just sat there, miserably, growing weaker and weaker during the two-hour crossing.

After landing in Stranraer Uncle Alex and his pals carried on the party on the train until they fell asleep in the early hours of the morning. I sat with the others in the RAF party from Northern Ireland, half-dead. Around about Carlisle I fell asleep, to be wakened later by Uncle Alex shaking me. It was dawn.

He was tall, very dark, with a good build and handsome features. Although he clearly had a bit of a hangover he nevertheless looked concerned for me as he bent over me. 'Are you OK?' he asked, 'we're getting off here.' I don't remember what station it was.

I told him yes I was OK. He squeezed my hand. 'Don't forget,' he said, 'stand well back on parade and volunteer for nothing.' With a final warm smile and wink he was off, and I was really on my own.

Uncle Alex had fondly imagined when he joined the Pioneers that he was going across to England to have a bit of a spree with the old brigade. What happened to him after he left me was that he spent a few weeks in England and was then shipped to France. He was there when the Germans broke through and he just made it to Dunkirk and home by the skin of his teeth.

However, I arrived, feeling very hard done by, at Padgate, Lancs, in mid-morning, 20 February. The sandwiches that Mother had made up for me – about the size of a two-pound loaf – were still in my suitcase. I remember feeling very homesick indeed, as I opened the package in some sort of RAF reception area, and bit into the fried egg sandwiches that Mother had wrapped so carefully back in Hillman Street.

My working-class Irish ignorance became apparent early in the proceedings. In the hut where our flight were to live an opinionated cockney corporal was handing out bedclothes to each of us in turn.

'Hey,' I said, after examining mine. 'I've got a sheet too many.' The corporal checked them. 'No you ain't,' he said, 'you got two there, you silly twit.'

'Yes,' I said, 'two. That's one too many.'

I genuinely couldn't understand it when the whole intake roared with laughter. I'd never seen more than one sheet in any of our beds at home in my life. That was when I learned that everybody else actually slept between two sheets. I also pulled off my greatest effort in self-control up to then. When that cockney corporal led the laughter I had the exact spot marked out on his receding chin that my knuckles were about to dinge, but I managed somehow to hold off and say nothing.

Lying in bed in Padgate that first night I felt really miserable. This was not the life for me, this regimented automaton's life, I reflected miserably. Why the hell hadn't I sailed away with Mart? I was never cut out for uniforms and short haircuts and drilling on the square, I thought. When I had been in bed awhile, I heard a train hoot in the distance, and I missed my home and family very badly indeed.

Then from the bottom of the hut in the darkness a wag of a Welshman began to tell jokes to the hut's inmates. I don't remember any except the last one, which went like this:

This guy was visiting someone in hospital and he was taken short for a pee. He couldn't read very well, so when he saw a door opening on to the hospital corridor marked 'Laboratory' he thought it was a lavatory, so in he went.

'This is a funny sort of a bog,' he said to himself inside the door. 'There's only bottles and test tubes. Ah well. I suppose hospitals are funny that way,' so he lifted down from a shelf a test tube that seemed already to have something in it, and began to pee into it.

Suddenly there was an unmerciful explosion. Bits of glass few everywhere. The door burst open and the chap was blown into the corridor. Immediately doctors and nurses by the dozen appeared.

'Good God, man,' cried a doctor on reaching him. 'Your left leg's been blown off.'

'Never mind my left leg, Doc,' said the dazed victim, 'away and find my right hand. You'll never guess what's in it!'

I always enjoyed a dirty story. That first night in the RAF I fell asleep smiling after all.

When we got up next morning it was all go. Sign for this, sign for that. Dental check-up. Medical check-up. FFI – drop your slacks; don't be shy. Hearing for the first time the FFI joke, as follows:

This sadistic medical officer on an FFI used to pick up each man's doings on the end of his walking cane. After he had examined it to see if it was free from infection – or FFI – he would give it a sharp slap with his cane, enjoy the discomfort of the victim, and move to the next man.

He came to this little meek-looking chap, lifted the

brute, studied it, tapped it sharply, dropped it. No response. The little man never moved a muscle.

Same again with the same wee man. Lift the lanyard. Sharp tap. No response.

Try again. This time he really belted it. No joy. Not a muscle moved.

'How on earth can you stand that without wincing as the others do?' asked the MO, with professional interest aroused.

'It's nae bother tae me, Doctor,' said the wee man. 'It's nae ma tool. It belongs tae yon poor bastard behind me.'

But the inoculations and vaccinations were to come. Especially the inoculations. I forget whether it was the ATT or the TAB, whatever they mean, but it was one or the other, that really laid me low. I turned out to be a reactor to it. A very violent reactor to it at that.

The inoculation hit all of us. We were walking around protecting our arms like mad, for two days. But me? I was nearly a hospital case. And it didn't go away in two days either. My arm was still up like a bap after four days. I still had to carry on with normal duties too.

On the fifth morning after being inoculated I simply couldn't bring myself to get up at reveille. I felt dreadful, so I lay on.

In came the self-important cockney corporal. 'Wot!' he yelled. 'Still in the pit.' I tried to explain that I felt very ill, but he wouldn't have it.

'You'll have to go to sick quarters and report sick,' he said, 'and hurry up about it you stoopid git.'

As he said this he nudged my sore left arm.

I happened to be struggling to get my trousers on at the

time. As soon as the Englishman touched the jangled complex of vibrating agony that was my left upper arm I let my trousers fall to the ground and made to hit him with my good right hand on the part of his chin that I had marked out on my first day in the RAF. It was just off the mark. He was lucky.

The commanding officer, after listening to witnesses who were all on my side, reckoned that there were faults on both sides, so I began my RAF career with fourteen days confined to barracks.

They took the corporal away from our flight after that. A good thing, too, I might have ended up doing twenty-one years for him.

I've never really been able to take to cockney Englishmen since that.

16

PRELUDE TO THE SLAUGHTER IV
THE CAST ASSEMBLES

The *Kenbane Head* sailed from Belfast on Thursday 12 September 1940 and arrived in Dublin next day, tying up at the North Wall.

A number of crew members got leave to travel back to Belfast by train on Saturday the 14th, under orders to return next day.

Leckey, the second mate, was going back to Belfast to see his newly-born baby, and Belshaw, the ship's carpenter, was going to Ballywalter to bury his wife's grandfather. They talked philosophically of life and death on the train going home.

Jim Emerson and Mart travelled back together and Billy McBride, one of the sailors, joined them. McBride was only going back to Belfast to pass the time – he didn't fancy Dublin much, and he didn't fancy the *Kenbane Head* much either. He and Mart had become pretty good pals. Mart's days of drinking shandy were over now and he joined McBride in a bottle of stout and a half 'un of whiskey in the restaurant car. Jim Emerson was with them because he went everywhere that Mart went.

By this time Mart was married and had a house almost

halfway between Maggie's people and his own – at 98 Hillman Street. His flying visit home was an unexpected treat for his wife of three months – or rather, since he had been at sea for most of the time since his marriage, his wife of about fourteen days.

They all returned on time and the *Kenbane Head* sailed on Monday 16 September for Fowey, in Cornwall, where she took on china clay for Three Rivers. By Saturday 21 September the *Kenbane Head* was in station with a westbound convoy, starting the fourteen-day, stomach-knotting voyage across the U-boats' playground. But they made it this time to the Straits of Belle Isle and safety.

When they had discharged the china clay at Three Rivers the deck crew were put to scrubbing and washing the hold on the way to Montreal. This was a job that they hated, but the hold had to be made ready for general cargo.

At least that was one good thing about it, they thought, as they washed and hosed; they would have a few days in Montreal, where the lights were much brighter than at home, and the grub was a whole lot better. They could buy nylons for wives and girlfriends, and relax in their favourite bars for a few days, before thoughts of the trip home began to ulcerate them once again.

It was well into October by the time the *Kenbane* was ready to sail to Halifax to join a convoy for home.

Back in Halifax, Nova Scotia, the *Jervis Bay* and her company had just returned after another uneventful convoy escort. The next convoy was not due to leave until 28 October. They had a few days to spare yet.

The *Jervis Bay*'s crew included a considerable number of ex–merchant navy men. Although they were in uniform, they continued to behave in the quiet, unobtrusive way that merchant seamen do when they are ashore. They were fond of a drink, and lots of them were over-fond of it perhaps, but they were not men to go roistering and wrecking and making their presence felt as the RNVR (Royal Naval Volunteer Reserve) ratings tended to do.

Not that there was much in Halifax for anybody to get excited about. The Nova Scotians were an undemonstrative lot who had seen it all too many times before. The people had taken on the bleak character of their habitat.

Anybody who felt like roistering in this place needed only to have the blank, bored gaze of a native Nova Scotian turned on him and the drink turned to soda water in his system. Not even John Wayne, Errol Flynn and the whole US Marine Corps could have put any fizz into Halifax. The place was purely functional. It was a harbour and roadstead for ships leaving Canada to carry war supplies to Britain. No more and no less.

So the *Jervis Bay*'s shore leave contingent didn't tend to rush up towards the town on their liberties. They walked, to put the time in, until the next milestone in the dull progression of their lives – the mustering and sailing of Convoy HX 84 for Britain.

Down in New York city a nineteen-year-old named Hugh Blair McCready was counting the days. He had left Belfast just before the outbreak of war to help look after the American interests of the Ulster textile firm of Ewarts Ltd.

The cool detachment of the Americans regarding the happenings in the old country during the 'phoney war' period had just about equalled McCready's own concern for events in Europe. He was in an exciting business atmosphere in New York and in addition, he could relax after working hours with the most generous and hospitable nation in the world.

But the calamity that had befallen British arms in the summer of 1940 had caused the Belfast boy to think again. Restlessness and then deep concern had hardened into resolution. Hugh McCready wanted to go home and join the armed forces.

Once his employers and family understood his conviction, they helped as best they could. Transatlantic travel was not easy to arrange, but the folks back home had heard that the Head Line had carried a few passengers on each trip in peacetime. Enquiries were made at the firm's head office in Victoria Street, Belfast.

Yes, the line still carried passengers. Yes, they would accept Hugh Blair McCready. Could he go to Montreal, Canada, from New York, by 20 October? Good. Thank you.

Oh. Just one thing. The name of the ship. It will be the *Kenbane Head*. K-E-N-B-A-N-E – *Kenbane Head*. OK? Good-day Sir.

Besides the *Kenbane Head* thirty-seven other ships that were either sailing or loading as October 1940 began to run out were to converge on Sydney and Halifax, Nova Scotia, to form Convoy HX 84.

Some of them were tankers. Floating firebombs. There was the *Erodona*, *Athel Empress*, *Delphinula*, *St Cobain*, *Sovac*, *Solfonn*, *San Demetrio*, *Cordelia*, *James J Maguire*, and *Athel Templar*.

Eleven tankers, all filled up and making their way to Halifax as October waned. These were the beauties that the

U-boats loved. Send a tanker up, and you get real job satisfaction, said the men of the *Unterseebooten*.

One of the greatest wonders of the Second World War was the fact that shipping companies were able to get seamen to sail in these vessels at all, for standard merchant navy pay.

One big ship was making its way up the east coast to join HX 84. The *Rangitiki*, 16,698 tons, pride of the New Zealand Shipping Company, with its two funnels, would be the most distinctive ship on parade, when HX 84 put to sea. She was carrying 10,000 tons of cheese, butter, meat and wool plus 75 passengers. It took a crew of 223 to work this ship, commanded by Captain Henry Barnett.

Captain Barnett, like all merchant seamen, was a man who liked to keep himself neat and spruce. Because his ship carried a large number of passengers his smart appearance was even more important. As the *Rangitiki* sailed towards Halifax captain and crew were models of dress and deportment. Mr A. Swift, the purser, and his staff of stewards and stewardesses were a credit to the company.

Passengers were reassured by orderliness. One lady passenger, Miss Ruth Shannon, who was coming to Britain to do war work, was to say when the *Rangitiki* reached port safely after a voyage that was hair-raising, to say the least: 'The service as usual was excellent.'

Freighters with foreign-sounding names like *Anna Bulgari*, *Varoy* and *Stureholm* were either at Halifax or on their way there. Others, like *Cornish City*, *Dan y Bryn*, *Trewellard*, and *Beaverford*, had a familiar, homely ring to their names.

Besides the Red Duster of the British merchant service a number of other flags were flown on vessels earmarked for the convoy. Two were Belgian, four were Swedish, four Norwegian, two Polish, and one Greek. All looking to the Royal Navy for protection during the voyage home.

Some authorities, in commenting on the security aspect of convoy organisation in Halifax, have pointed out that the German Admiralty were put in prompt possession of the relevant details by intelligence agents based in the seaport. The shore activity of ships' masters going to convoy briefing at roughly the same time, with busy comings and goings of taxis, has been blamed as one of several careless touches which alerted the German agents.

In fact the whole town of Halifax knew when a convoy was assembling because they could see it doing so. The only function of the port in wartime was to accommodate vessels leaving for, or arriving from, Britain.

The trick was to keep the route of the convoy a secret from the Germans. This the Admiralty managed to do throughout the war.

But of course there's not much point in feeling smug because you've kept a convoy route secret when there's a chance that the enemy will find a way to mount a wide search pattern from any point roughly ahead of the convoy, is there?

'Aha,' the port admiral might have said if you had raised the point in October 1940, 'but it would take a ship to move at a hell of a speed to cover an area sufficiently wide to be sure of finding the convoy. Like 120 knots, maybe?' This with a sly smile.

'But what,' omniscient, you might have said to the admiral, 'if the ship carries an aeroplane that flies at precisely that speed? One with floats? One that can be put down on the sea and lifted up again, as needed?'

'Like an Arado 196 maybe?' the admiral might have replied, and dissolved into fits of laughter.

On board the pocket battleship *Admiral Scheer* they called the Arado 196 the Parrot, because of its drooped nose. The Parrot and its pilot were safely tucked up on board when the *Scheer*'s moorings were cast off and the lean warship powered its way out of the Baltic port of Gdynia. It was 23 October 1940.

The radar had been tested and was working perfectly. The crew were battle-ready. Her supply ship *Nordmark* had sailed six days earlier with instructions to sail to a position south of Jan Mayen Island at latitude 70° N. On reaching this position the *Nordmark* was to sail westwards on the edge of the ice. Calculating its course precisely, the supply ship passed the narrowest point of the Denmark Strait in darkness. By 27 October the *Nordmark* had reached the North Atlantic.

Following precisely the same headings *Scheer* followed her supply ship six days later. Her captain, Theodor Krancke, was under orders 'to relieve pressure on German operations in the North Sea and English Channel by rapid action which would tend to upset normal dispositions of British escort forces'.

He was to commence this operation by attacking one of the inadequately escorted convoys from Canada to Britain.

Then he was to choose targets of opportunity as these presented themselves.

But he was not permitted to risk his ship against anything even approaching equal firepower and manoeuvrability. The lesson of the *Graf Spee* was still fresh in Krancke's mind.

The pocket battleship *Graf Spee*, sister-ship to the *Scheer*, had already been in position in the South Atlantic when war broke out. She had already sunk nine ships when she was sighted by a British cruiser squadron 150 miles east of the River Plate on 13 December 1939.

The cruisers, *Exeter*, *Ajax* and *Achilles*, collectively, had less firepower in their 6-inch guns than the *Graf Spee* packed in her 11-inch broadsides. Early in the action *Exeter* suffered heavy damage and after just over an hour she had to break off with both forward and after turrets out of action, serious fires raging, a heavy list, and eighty-four casualties, including sixty-one dead.

Ajax and *Achilles* kept harassing the *Graf Spee*, despite the fact that *Ajax* had lost the use of five of her eight 6-inch guns. *Graf Spee* was hit no less than twenty-seven times by the more lightly-armed British ships. Thirty-six of her men were killed and sixty were wounded. The pocket battleship was utterly unable to shake off her pursuers and eventually Captain Hans Langsdorff, with the eyes of the world on him, sailed his ship into the Uruguayan port of Montevideo.

Outside the mouth of the Plate *Ajax*, *Achilles* and the newly-arrived cruiser *Cumberland* patrolled patiently, whilst Langsdorff's men laboured to make the *Graf Spee* ready for sea in the seventy-two hours that the Uruguayan government had allotted for the task.

At the same time the British began a propaganda war of nerves, issuing carefully disseminated reports that heavy reinforcements were just over the horizon.

Eight-five minutes before the end of the time limit Captain Langsdorff scuttled his ship seven miles outside Montevideo harbour, before the eyes of thousands of sightseers. The order to scuttle the *Graf Spee* had been given directly by Hitler.

On 18 December Langsdorff, considering himself branded a coward, shot himself in his hotel room. The High Command publicly approved his suicide.

Theodor Krancke had no wish to repeat Langsdorff's experience. His was to be a hit-and-run mission. But his men were ready just in case: 'If we have to fight,' Krancke told them before sailing, 'then let each man on board this ship do his duty, in the spirit of the great sailor whose name it bears.'

On 27 October the *Scheer* entered Kiel Canal and emerged into the Elbe protected by destroyers and fighter planes. By 28 October after taking cover in a fjord near Stavanger in Norway, with fighter screen overhead, the *Scheer* set course for the Denmark Strait.

Entering the strait in rough weather many of the Germans were seasick. Krancke was keeping unbroken watch on the bridge or in the charthouse. A plane was sighted, but it turned out to be a Dornier 18.

On 30 October the weather turned really vile. No one could go on deck without being roped. A bo'sun and an AB were lost overboard.

A few hours after passing the narrowest part of the strait,

on 31 October, a ship was sighted six to seven thousand yards away. This was probably an armed merchant cruiser on the Northern Patrol. She failed to see the pocket battleship.

Thus the British naval blockade was evaded. There was also supposed to be a constant RAF watch on these waters, but this, too, was ineffective. In defence both of the Navy and the RAF, however, it must be said that Britain had not dropped her guard against invasion and a considerable element of her air and sea forces had been detailed to reconnoitre the continental ports for signs of activity in this direction.

By 2 November Krancke had broken through into the North Atlantic. His ship was in the area known as the Black Pit, not covered by air patrols.

The battleship *Scheer* prepared to search the area 52–54° N, 32–35° W. All lookouts were warned to be vigilant.

The 'B' Service, which monitored radio broadcasts from British shipping, reported to Krancke that two convoys were due to pass through the *Scheer*'s operational area.

On 3 November the engine of the Arado was being run up. The Parrot would be needed in a couple of days.

Thus all the cast was assembled. The *Jervis Bay*, the convoy and the battleship *Scheer*.

There remains only one more ship to be mentioned.

The *Mopan*, an Elder and Fyffe's banana boat. An ordinary banana boat. Yet it had a critical role in the coming drama.

This ship might have warned the *Jervis Bay* that the *Scheer* was intercepting. But it didn't.

On the other hand, this ship, to a far greater degree than Fogarty Fegen or the *Jervis Bay*, was instrumental in saving most of the ships in Convoy HX 84.

17
LEARNING A TRADE

When I was a kid I used to love to read the popular magazines that featured First World War flying stories. Often these yarns included a reference to the hero's favourite rigger:

> The rigger threw Chichester a glance of reproach: 'Your aerobatics 'ave made a couple of these 'ere flying wires part, sir,' he said, 'I doubt if I can have this 'ere aeroplane ready in time for the dawn patrol.'
>
> Chichester pulled off his helmet and ran his fingers through his thick blonde hair: 'Come, come, Hawkins, old chap,' he smiled, 'You've tidied the old girl up when she was a lot worse than this. And in a couple of jiffies too. Set to, my dear fellow. See you in the morning.' The skipper of 95 Squadron set off back to the flight hut, leaving his rigger staring gloomily at the tattered, bullet-riddled fabric of the Bristol Bulldog.

The RAF didn't appear to have advanced much beyond this romantic state when I, somewhat thankfully, shook the dust of Padgate, Lancs, off my feet and arrived, with about fifty flight riggers and flight mechanics under training, at RAF station St Athan, Glamorgan.

The course of instruction began in mid-April 1940 and was to last eighteen weeks. I learned to splice a wire and do the herringbone stitch when repairing torn fabric. I learned when to pull the chocks away and how to salute the pilot from the wingtip when he was ready to taxi for take-off.

They taught me how to cooperate with the pilot in starting an aeroplane engine. Hand on the airscrew (never call it a propeller). Shout: 'Switches off. Petrol on. Throttle closed. Suck in!' and then swing the airscrew clockwise.

And then one day – I did it. I yelled 'Contact', pulled the airscrew round and she started up. Just like the magazine stories!

Big deal, said I.

The course nearly defeated me at the very first stage, not surprisingly known as Basic Training. We were each handed a gnarled, misshapen lump of mild steel and a bastard file. The idea was to file the thing down to a perfect cube. But perfect.

Why on earth some people should be able to file metal evenly and others should find it impossible baffles me to this day. In my case the effort was a complete disaster. I positioned my feet the way I had been told; I placed the second, third and fourth fingers of my left hand on top of the file, exerting slight pressure, and I took care to keep the file level as I moved it back and forward. My finished product was even more misshapen than the piece of rough steel I had started with. The moon-faced Welsh civilian instructor told me that it was the worst effort he had ever seen in his life, and before he even had the words out I told him that it was also the worst effort I had ever seen in my own life, never mind him.

Fashioning the cube wasn't the end of it. We then had to file down a piece of quarter-inch mild steel plate to a size one-inch all round wider than the cube. Then – and I remember wondering whether I was experiencing a nightmare when the instructor gave us the news – we had to file a precisely square hole in the middle of the plate. The cube was to fit into the hole with only a slight press. The joint was to be tight.

I was never in my life a quitter. I had a go at it. When the instructor saw the finished job he looked at me in awe. 'Did you do this on purpose?' he asked. I nodded. He led me to the door of the hangar. With his arm on my shoulder he pointed to a small party of airmen in blue fatigues who were painting gas-warning signs by the roadside.

'Those airmen all came here hoping to become riggers or mechanics,' the instructor said in his nasal Cardiff accent, 'they all failed. They are now aircrafthands, general duty. For perhaps the rest of their lives these lost souls will wander from one aerodrome to another, painting gas-warning signs. Get it?' I nodded dumbly. 'Then get bloody back in there and get filing!' he yelled.

It wasn't all work, of course. RAF St Athan was still run on peacetime lines up to the fall of France. Wednesday afternoons were set aside for sport, and long weekend passes were easy to come by. For those, like myself, who lived too far away to go home and back in a weekend, Saturdays and Sundays were spent lazing comfortably about the camp.

It puzzled me for about a month that our hut emptied completely on Saturday afternoons. 'Where on earth does everybody go?' I asked one of my course-mates after my fourth lonely Saturday. 'Down to the Four Bells,' he said. It was located in a hamlet with a name like Cowslip Major or something.

It is a measure of my innocence at the time that the pub was the last place to enter my mind, as a way of passing a Saturday afternoon.

It entered my head easily enough once it got the chance in early May, I can tell you that much. I didn't waste any time mooning about the camp the following, or any more Saturday afternoons. My first drink in the Four Bells pub was a pint. I sank it straight down without taking it from my head, in response to a challenge by a Scotsman from Skye.

'That's the way to take it,' I said, thinking of Uncle Alex, 'branches and all.'

That afternoon we treated ourselves well. The other lads in the group felt bound to explain to me, as we swayed campwards at 6 p.m., that they had never drunk so much beer on their previous Saturday afternoon sessions. Today they had made an exception.

This was a phenomenon with which I became gradually more familiar as my months in the RAF increased. Whenever I joined with a company of Britishers in a drinking bout they suddenly found themselves drinking like Irishmen which is to say without rhyme, reason or regard for money.

When we arrived back in the cookhouse that Saturday the duty corporal cook refused at first to serve us. 'Tea's over,' he said flatly, 'you're too late.'

'Come around this side of the counter and say that,' I told

him, beerily, hunching my thin shoulders, 'and I'll hammer you into the floor like a nail.'

Seven days' jankers that remark cost me, but I had at one and the same time become a character and a ringleader, and I was very rarely lonely for the remainder of my time on that station. Not now that I'd discovered beer.

I had my first ever 'flip' as we called it, in an aeroplane at the time when the British troops were being evacuated from the Channel ports. From the back seat of a Miles Magister I saw from two thousand feet a large convoy of ships approaching Barry, but I had no idea of its significance at the time. Indeed, although the news from France and Belgium had been bad for some time, I scarcely paid any attention to it. I had literally no interest in the war.

The flight in the Magister affected me most profoundly. I had experienced some trepidation before take-off, but once I was in the air I hardly stopped screwing my head and shoulders around, eager to see everything, looking down over the aircraft's side, then up, then all around. It was the most unbelievably marvellous feeling I had ever experienced. The ships in the Bristol Channel looked like children's toys, moving with clockwork motors along the edge of a village pond.

'Can you loop the loop?' I shouted down the speaking tube. The pilot shook his head. A moment later, to ease my disappointment, he put the Magister into a steep dive right over the ships, then he pulled back on the stick and I felt my cheeks sag and my mouth fall open as I knew for the first time the helpless paralysis that lies at the bottom of every dive.

When we landed the airfield was buzzing with activity.

Troop carriers were disgorging soldiers, dishevelled and without their arms. Some of the troops were in foreign uniforms. Hatless officers and NCOs (non-commissioned officers) were falling groups of soldiers into line and marching them off.

I tried to coax the sergeant pilot into taking me up again, but it was no go. The circuit was alive with planes of all sizes.

It was about 2 June that I had my first flight, because the evacuation of the troops from France had only a couple more days to run. They brought hundreds of Tommies on to St Athan and we trainee riggers and mechanics gladly gave up our huts and beds to them whilst we made ourselves comfortable on the floor of the gym.

On the first night that our troops arrived on the station we bought them beer for as long as our money lasted. Our feeling of pity for them was intense.

Then as soon as they got drunk, the soldiers turned on us: 'Where the hell were the Brylcreem boys at Dunkirk?' they wanted to know. As if we could tell them. Hardly any of us even bothered reading the papers.

One diminutive, snaggle-toothed Glaswegian handed me an uppercut to the snout, when I tried to reason with him. 'Why should we fall out?' I had been saying. 'We're comrades-in-arms, aren't we?'

Just with that he let me have it. 'Hell roast ye, ye Army bastard ye,' I yelled, the blood running out of me. I let him have one to the mouth, Dunkirk or no Dunkirk, and the next thing I knew a soldier who seemed as big as Carnera had me in a bear hug and would have killed me if I hadn't taken a grip of his particulars in the way that I had learned in Cosgrave Street.

That was a bad night for RAF St Athan, but I expect it made the British Expeditionary Force feel better. A victory's a victory, even if it's only over riggers and mechanics. But I was to see the same syndrome in later years anyway, out in Cairo and Alexandria. Every time the Army got a hiding from Jerry the poor old RAF got beaten up.

'We are the boys in blue,' we used to say. 'Black and friggin' blue!'

On Saturday 22 June 1940, for some reason – probably financial – I arrived back in camp from the Four Bells earlier than usual.

'Hey Paddy,' somebody told me, 'there's a telegram for you at the camp post office.'

Telegram? Good God, I thought. Mart! I ran as hard as I could. The corporal postman winked as he handed me the envelope. 'Any chance of a beer tonight, Paddy?' he joked. I was outside, looked at the envelope, 978579 AC 2 McAughtry, it read. No clue from that. I opened it.

Inside was a telegraphic money order for one pound, and a message on the side.

'Just married,' it said. 'Good luck. Marriott.'

Our lovely Mart. He thought of me on his wedding day: and me away over in Wales. I walked slowly back towards my hut, and before I could stop myself, I cried. Christ, he was a marvellous bloke. Imagine taking the time to go to the post office and everything on his wedding day. I had been four months away from home and to tell the truth I hadn't been in the habit of thinking much about it after a couple of weeks or so. But, that afternoon, on the way to my hut, and then lying on my bed, I would have given anything, anything at all, just to have five minutes with Mart. Just to see him. On his wedding day. I'll bet he looked smashing. And Maggie Keel too. Oh Mart, Mart ... I was back to the time when I was a kid, and his ship was putting to sea. I cried long and sore for him.

The final examinations were held in late July. Under 40 per cent was a fail mark; 40 to 60 was AC 2; and 60 to 80 was AC 1. Over 80 per cent and you were sent to the bench to do a wire splice. This meant that you had only to complete the splice and you were a leading aircraftman.

I managed 41 per cent. I was an aircraftman second class with a trade. I was a flight rigger. I was delighted with myself.

One more thing happened before I left St Athan. Attached to the station was an air navigation school and as a consequence the circuit was usually pretty busy. The day before we left a Blenheim bomber joined the circuit. It made such a change from the Avro Anson trainers which made up the station's complement that most of those out and about the camp that day stopped to look at it.

It looked so efficient and warlike, that Blenheim bomber, compared to the lumbering trainers. We stood admiring its businesslike lines. Suddenly it pulled out of the circuit, flew right across to the centre of the camp and dropped a stick of whistling bombs right across the hutments. As neat as you like!

The air raid killed a few of the lads, I think. But for years after that, whenever I mentioned to an old St Athan-ite that I had been there in 1940, I was always asked: 'Were you there when the Blenheim bombed the camp?' It was a sort of datum point.

Well, I was there when the Blenheim bombed the camp. I remember it well. It was the first time I really learned that a man could lose control of his bowels with fright.

No. It wasn't me. It was a Welshman. A flight mechanic from Blaina. I won't mention his name.

It could happen to a bishop.

I went with a small detachment of riggers and mechanics to RAF Cranfield in Bedfordshire. No. 14 Service Flying Training School.

On leaving St Athan I had amassed a few days confinement to barracks and loss of privileges. On entering Cranfield I made a vow to myself that I would turn over a new leaf. I dumped my stuff on the bed and, mug in hand, set off for the cookhouse, whistling merrily. Out of the way there, I was thinking. There's a tradesman coming …

'Airman!' I stopped dead, resignedly. What the hell was it this time? A tall lean corporal of the service police came up from behind. He was immaculate. He shimmered, so highly polished was he.

I was to get to know this man well. He looked at me with distaste – 'Haircut,' he rapped out. 'Get a haircut.' He looked at my tunic. 'Buttons. Filthy.' Stepping back, he looked at my feet. 'Shoes. Filthy,' he said, with tight lips.

'What's your name?' he asked, looking at me as if I was a piece of dog's dirt carried in on his shoe.

'McAughtry, Corporal,' I said.

'Christ,' he said, 'a bullshitting Irishman.'

I sighed.

'Away and frig yourself, Corporal,' I said.

As usual I had settled in quickly.

18

THE TURNING POINT

While the Battle of Britain raged in the south of England we riggers and mechanics down at the flights often found ourselves with time on our hands after our training aircraft went up. We used to assemble at the dispersals or outside the hangars, setting up card schools, or maybe pitch-and-toss. Sometimes we just lazed the sunny hours away.

It was at this time that I had a magnificent scrap with an electrician named Hartshorn, who came from Durham or thereabouts.

He was a guy with a very cutting tongue. Most people let him away with it because he also had a bad temper. He was big and raw-boned, and had a violent look about him. I suppose there was bound to be trouble between us one day, for my own tongue wasn't all that disciplined.

This Hartshorn started imitating my Ulster talk one day. He had a big audience. I still wasn't any happier about being laughed at than I had ever been, so, after deciding that the man was working his way up to war, I whipped my forage cap off and let him have the badge end up the gub.

Before the blitz started I said to myself you've done it this time all right Sam. Those big gnarled knuckles'll just about dunder you from Bedfordshire to Carrickfergus and back at his pleasure.

I wasn't far wrong, at that. Boom! Down on the flat of my back. Splat! How the hell did I get that one? Bang! One on the side of the jaw. Your mouth was hanging slack when that one landed, Sam. You'll know all about that one in the morning. Why do I feel so sleepy?

After hoisting myself to my feet for about the fourth time I made an interesting discovery. Hartshorn had no puff left. And, sore as I was, I still had. I managed to disfigure him just as badly as he had done me before we both fell to the cool grass, useless and spent.

My nose was broken in that one. It affected my hearing in later years. But that fight drew a lot of attention on the station. For one thing it changed the attitude of one or two of the more sadistic policemen, and both Hartshorn and I were largely left alone when sacrificial lambs were being sought by the guardroom boys.

In September we got a brand new recruit in the flight. He was the first of a new breed. The RAF had decided to bring all trainee pilots and observers in as leading aircraftmen instead of sergeants or officers, whilst they were being trained.

This new man of ours had agreed to come into the service as a general duty aircrafthand, until a backlog of applicants was dealt with, and he could be sent to navigation school to begin his observer's course. His job on the flight was to book the aircraft up and down and generally to record movements and serviceability.

I was immediately interested in this fellow. His mind was lively and he seemed to be stuffed with knowledge of all kinds.

He read books. Interesting books. I edged up close to him one day to see the title of one of them. *Air Navigation* it was called. It had an Air Ministry crest on the cover.

He smiled at my interest and began to explain to me the little that he knew of the ancient science of navigation.

I was fascinated. The application of navigation to seafaring made it certain that this subject would grip me. Together with this chap, whose name I completely forget now, I spent many brow-wrinkling hours poring over that primer. Gradually I began to find sense in the thing.

I began to go up in the Oxfords then, in order to try out map reading. I would sit by myself on the main spar, without benefit of intercom, studying a borrowed map, trying to pinpoint our position by peering out of the window by the door.

At the end of September my fellow student was whisked away to navigation school, but I kept flying when I could, and borrowed a copy of the air navigation book for my own use. It was hard going for me. I had never heard of parallelograms of forces, or vector triangles. I had to screw my eyes up pretty hard to understand the difference between compass variation and deviation and to fathom the distinction between the true course, the magnetic course, and the compass course. Air speed and ground speed, wind velocity and dead-reckoning positions. Such a lot to understand. I loved trying.

One day, after I had landed and was walking back to the flight with the pilot – a flight lieutenant – he asked me whether I might be interested in doing a pilot's course.

'You might as well get paid for all the flying you do,' he finished smiling.

I looked at him in astonishment. Pilots were young gods to me, whether they were trained or not. They were educated and they were cultured. They mixed naturally with brother officers or sergeants. From snatches of their talk that I had heard, they all seemed to be extremely clever, not to say witty. I imagined them all to be sons of doctors, or solicitors, or architects. They certainly looked it. So had the observers I had seen being trained at St Athan.

'I could never be a pilot, sir,' I told the officer. 'I'm not smart enough.'

'Rubbish,' he said briskly. 'Think about it.'

Shove that one up your bloody nose, corporal of police, I said to myself. Just look out, old son. I've got friends in high places. But it was only a dream. I kept flying and studying, but only as a sort of hobby. It was better than playing poker for cigarettes.

It was at the end of September that Kesselring began to admit that the RAF were superior to the Luftwaffe over Britain. Air ace Galland was telling Goering that he would like an outfit of Spitfires for his group, and over by Cranfield, Bucks, I was pretty brassed off with Jake Thomson ...

WAAFs (Women's Auxiliary Air Force) were beginning to arrive in numbers and I had organised myself with one the very minute she arrived, uncertainly, in the canteen, with a couple of her mates.

'The name is Derek Henderson,' I said, swooping to her side. She was a Free Stater, name of Deirdre. I took to her in a big way. She was dark, with deep blue eyes, pageboy bob, and a slim figure. She liked the Belfast tongue, she told me. Deirdre herself came from Limerick.

I used the name Derek Henderson every time I tried to make it with the girls, reckoning it to be a name with an easy flow to it. 'As sure as my name's Derek Henderson' I used to say several times a night, to make sure the bint had it well and truly lodged in the old brain.

I met Deirdre the next night outside the Waffery as arranged, took her for a walk and then brought her into the pub for a drink with three bob in my pocket. She ordered a gin.

'Don't order any more gins or I'll murder you, as sure as my name's Derek Henderson,' I said to her, laughing, as I thought, easily.

'Sure your name's not Derek Henderson,' said Deirdre. 'Why do you keep saying it is?'

'What the … what the divil are you talkin' about,' I blustered. 'Not Derek Henderson? Not bloody half Derek Henderson.' I was in some confusion.

'What's the matter with your own name?' she asked. 'Sam's a good name. There's nothing at all wrong with Sam.'

By this time I was burning with slow mortification. 'Who told you my name was Sam,' I wanted to know.

'The chap who was with you last night, when you went up to the counter for two wads and two teas for you and me,' she said.

'Man, Thomson, but you're a great frigpot,' I said to Jake Thomson next day, back in the camp.

'It has tae be done, Paddy,' he said, showing his snaggle teeth in what he obviously imagined to be a smile. 'All's fair in love and war.'

'Anyway,' he said, 'you were never in with a chance. The wee lassie's fonder o' somebody else than she is of you.'

'Who?' I wanted to know.

'Austin MacLeod from the Isle of Skye,' he said.

'Who, in the name of Jasus, is Austin MacLeod from the Isle of Skye?' I asked in bewilderment.

'Me,' said Jake Thomson, with an evil wink.

As that golden September of 1940 faded into grey October a very close friend of mine had two experiences that marked a turning point for him. In fact you could say it made a man of him, instead of a nineteen-year-old innocent.

This close friend was a Belfastman. He was a tall, thin rigger, with a slightly deviated septum brought on by way of a fight with an ignorant big Geordie name of Hartshorn …

My friend's name was Sam. A Scotsman named Joe Walsh and he were drinking in a village near their RAF camp. Joe was in civilian digs with a bachelor of about fifty, and he's the one who was doing the buying. Already Sam had had about eight pints. He was worried.

'I'm worried,' he confessed to Joe Walsh and his landlord. They wanted to know why.

'I'm in civilian digs with an old lady and her daughter,' Sam told them. 'They won't be too keen on their lodger landing in with a cargo of pints on board,' he said.

'Why don't you stop over with us?' Joe's landlord said. 'I'll bring some beer back.' There was no need to persuade Sam. This was like pushing an open door.

Between them they murdered a dozen or so of bottles, then they had some grub, and it was time for bed. 'You'll have to bunk up with me, I'm afraid, Sam,' Joe's landlord said. Sam shrugged. It was all one to him. He undressed, tumbled into bed, and listened with polite drowsiness to the landlord rambling on about the wound he had sustained in the First War. Then he dropped into a deep, beery sleep.

Some time in the early hours of the morning he awoke in a cold sweat. Terror was more like it. He was in paralysis. It was a nightmare.

The guy's hands were roaming all over him. He was an arsey versey!

Suddenly, somehow, Sam managed to move. He sat bolt upright. His elbow, flung savagely sideways, caught the older man on the head. Sam scrambled over him and made it to the light switch. The landlord sat up in the bright light, rubbing his eyes, pretending to have just awoken. 'What's the trouble, Paddy,' he asked, rubbing his face where Sam's elbow had caught him. Sam didn't answer. All he wanted to do was get out of there as fast as he could. He hared out of the house, got on to the road, and walked it back to camp, footsore and weary, but, he told himself, virgo intacta, at least.

After that Sam decided to keep off the beer for a while. He didn't want to run into the wounded soldier again. He told himself though, that it wouldn't be hard to work out where he had been wounded in the war ...

In his own quiet, semi-detached billet he settled down after that to a programme of early evenings. The old lady had a soft spot for Sam because he had brought her back a couple of pigs' knees from Belfast, provided by his Uncle Sammy, who worked as a knife man in Sinclair's bacon factory.

The daughter, Martha, and he had become friendly too. She was about two years older than himself, and worked in a solicitor's office. Martha was educated all right. In pursuance of his hobby of navigation Sam was by now doing maths and he was having problems with logarithms.

Martha showed him how to do the logs during those evenings in early October, while her mother made Marmite sandwiches for them. Sam talked a lot to Martha, mostly lies. He told her all about the ships he had sailed in, as apprentice, and about the big house that an uncle had left him in his will. He had already explained to Martha that his father was a master mariner, and that his mother's people owned a small shipping company called the Head Line. Uncle Thomas was the managing director, he explained.

Martha was a big girl, and motherly in her ways. Sam felt very comfortable with her. She had Germanic blonde hair and blue eyes. She had what are called good proportions. Martha was a great listener, and a good teacher too.

Sam found himself telling her, for some mad reason, that his maternal grandmother lived in a lighthouse on Benbecula. 'And her owning a shipping company and all?' Martha asked, in wonder.

'Money turns some people's heads,' Sam told her earnestly. He was a terrible liar.

The programme of early evenings had lasted about five days. Sam went up to his room early one night, explaining to the ladies that they needn't worry if they heard him moving about. He wanted to work at his maths he told them.

In half an hour the old woman and her daughter had retired to their separate rooms, and Sam gradually became lost in the problems he was working on. It must have been a good hour further on when the door opened quietly. It was Martha, holding her finger to her lips.

She wore a flowered housecoat. She closed the door silently. Sam was lying on top of the bed, dressed only in his pyjama bottoms. His books and papers were scattered all over the bed.

As Martha came over to the bed her housecoat parted, and he saw her bare leg, exposed well up the thigh. A very well-proportioned bare leg it was, too. His mouth suddenly went bone dry.

'Move over,' she said, bending over him and smiling a little. He saw that she looked nervous too. 'Certainly. Yes,' Sam said. His voice came out badly cracked. 'I'll just move my trig tables ...' and, in a totter of nerves he fumbled the papers off the top of the bed. He had never in his life seen so much of a girl's leg.

Martha slipped into his bed, still wearing the housecoat. Standing over her all Sam could see was her bosom. He was shaking. Never had he felt so overcome, and yet, at the same time, so thrilled and excited.

'Come on, Christopher Columbus,' said Martha, calmer now, patting the place beside her. The housecoat fell open further. God in heaven take care of us. They were huge! They were giant-sized! They were magnificently marvellously scrumptiously beautifully smashing. Sam thought something inside him was going to explode.

By this time he couldn't even speak. He just stood there. His eyes were sitting out like dogs' clinkers, as you might say.

Martha got out of bed, put out the light, got back into bed, and gently drew Sam in beside her. She had unbuttoned the housecoat in the darkness.

Sam couldn't even breathe. She whispered, close to him: 'For God's sake don't make a noise. Mother's a light sleeper.' But there was no hope of Sam making a noise, for Martha took his head and pulled it on to her bosom. For the first time Sam put his arms around her. Sense began to return. This is a peach of a woman, he thought, but at first she still had to tell him what to do. He knew everything in theory, but Martha had to let him know that it was OK to put it into practice.

After that shaky start, it seemed no time at all till Sam was whispering reminders to Martha to keep quiet for God's sake, or she would wake the old lady up …

This was the turning point of the Battle of Britain for Sam, just as it was for old Kesselring over there on the mat in front of Goering. Only Sam was enjoying it far more than Kesselring. And so did Martha, by golly. So did Martha.

Around about four in the morning they were lying contentedly, side by side.

'This is the only way to learn logs,' said Martha.

'It's a funny thing,' Sam told her. 'Only last week some bloke not a mile from here was trying to teach me something else. He was fond of the night shift too.'

'Teach you what?' asked Martha, starting to enfold him entirely.

'I suppose you could call it antilogs,' Sam said, from the depths.

19

THE SLAUGHTER I
THE ATTACK ON THE CONVOY

The main consideration in devising the formation of a convoy was to reduce as far as possible the area in which ships could be attacked from the flanks. The columns therefore sailed in broad lines abreast. The thirty-eight ships in Convoy HX 84 had sailed eastward at 1600 hours on Monday 20 October 1940 from Halifax in nine columns and four rows, with two extra merchantmen upsetting the exact symmetry of the design.

The first nine ships in order from north to south were the tanker *Eredona,* the *Andalusian,* the Norwegian *Hjalmar Wessel,* the *Empire Penguin,* the commodore's ship *Cornish City,* the *Rangitiki,* the *Trewellard,* the tankers *San Demetrio* and *James J Maguire.*

Steaming behind these were the Belgians *Emile Franqui* and *Persier,* the Norwegian *Cerus,* the Swedes *Stureholm* and *Vingaland,* the tankers *Delphinula* and *Sevac,* the *Maidan* and the tanker *Athel Templar.* The next nine were the Belgian *Danae II,* the *Fresco City,* the *Castilian,* the *Briar Wood,* the tanker *Athel Empress,* the *Pacific Enterprise,* the *Beaverford,* the tanker *Cordelia* and the Greek *Anna Bulgari.* There had been another ship in this row, the Polish *Morska Wola,* but on 1 November she had dropped behind because of engine trouble.

The rear column was made up of ten ships: the Swede *Delhi*, the *Lancaster Castle*, *Dan y Bryn*, the tanker *Oil Reliance*, the *Trefusis*, the tiny Polish ship *Puck*, just one thousand tons, the Swedish tanker *St Gobain*, the Norwegian tanker *Solfona*, the Norwegian freighter *Varcy*, and finally, last ship at the back of the column, the *Kenbane Head*.

The AMC *Jervis Bay* was out ahead of the convoy, sailing with the *Empire Penguin* and *Cornish City* on her port and starboard quarters respectively. Two Canadian destroyers had accompanied HX 84 for two days and then turned about for Halifax, leaving the *Jervis Bay* alone in charge.

By 5 November each ship in the convoy had settled to a well-drilled routine, keeping station four hundred yards from the ship ahead and six hundred yards from the one on either side.

Just before noon the lookout on the *Kenbane Head* and the other ships in the southern wing of the convoy were suddenly alert. Smoke was seen to the south-west. Soon eyes were glued to binoculars as the masts and superstructure of the stranger grew more visible.

She had a good four knots in hand of the seven-knot convoy. As the new arrival came up and then passed the convoy she was identified as the banana boat *Mopan*, 5,400 tons, making her way independently to Britain.

Gradually the *Mopan* drew ahead of the convoy and disappeared. HX 84 was alone again in the grey North Atlantic.

★

At just before 1000 hours that morning the *Admiral Scheer* sent its aircraft up, with Lieutenant Pietsch at the controls and an observer named Gallinat in the back seat.

The *Scheer's* search had brought her to the rough area 54° N and 32° W. 'Carry out a line-ahead search to the westward,' Krancke ordered the pilot. For forty minutes the Arado flew a search course as ordered, but drew a blank and returned to land alongside the *Scheer* at 1120 hours.

'Try searching to the south,' Krancke told Pietsch and the Parrot was lowered once again, to roar and bounce across the waves before lifting off to bank steeply, eager to find the convoy that the Germans knew to be somewhere near.

The whole ship's company of the *Scheer* was impatient for action. Already Krancke had allowed two distant merchantmen to escape because he feared to risk a radioed warning to the convoy. The *Scheer* was out for big pickings, it seemed.

Suddenly the Arado appeared overhead, twenty minutes earlier than expected. The observer was flashing a message in morse. 'Eighty-eight sea miles.' The time was 1240 hours.

By the time the aircraft was lifted back on board it was 1300 hours. Krancke learned from the pilot that he had sighted eight ships. Obviously this was only part of a large convoy. The *Scheer* had found her target.

Calculating that he could be up with the convoy by 1600 hours, Krancke ordered full speed ahead. He knew that he must waste no time at all if he was to do the maximum damage before nightfall.

Before setting course at 1300 hours Krancke had considered the consequences of a delay in engaging the British ships. This was the quarter-moon. Darkness fell early at this time of the year. Might it not be better to shadow the convoy using radar, and fall upon it just after dawn?

Krancke rejected this on the grounds that, by dawn next day, the convoy would be a hundred miles closer to home, and, more important, within two hundred miles of the area where he believed the escorts waited to bring the convoy on the last leg home.

His reasoning is important here. Krancke claimed that German intelligence did not know exactly where the Western Approaches escort vessels were stationed. This seems most improbable. The U-boats must surely have gained this information almost to the very yard!

The convoy was almost exactly halfway home when the *Scheer's* aircraft spotted it. The distance still to run was around a thousand miles. Even at the most pessimistic guess, the convoy would still have been many hundreds of miles away from the Western Approaches by dawn on 6 November.

Krancke also feared that a dawn attack next day might bring fast cruisers to the spot within six hours. But his ship was capable of twenty-seven knots. Even if he had been accurate in his guess of the whereabouts of the escorts, he had little to worry about. No cruiser could have come near him, after giving him a start of six hours in the broad wastes of the North Atlantic, and allowing for the absence of aircraft and radar on the British warships.

Bearing in mind Krancke's tight schedule for the convoy attack, his reasons for rejecting a dawn action hardly measure up to the standard of a man chosen to command the Naval Academy and later to take operational charge of the preparations for the sea campaign against Norway.

But even more inexplicable tactics by Krancke were to follow. For, at 1430 hours the *Scheer* came upon the banana boat *Mopan*.

This was most unexpected. The *Scheer* was already prepared for action. Her deck rails had been removed, the scuttles were screwed tight and heavy coverings were screwed into place. Below decks, pictures had been taken off the bulkheads. Krancke was certainly not expecting a lone ship. The aircraft seemed to have missed this vessel on its second search.

Krancke was suspicious. Was it an AMC? As the two ships closed it was obvious that the merchantman was too small to be an auxiliary cruiser – she only looked to be about six thousand tons. Nevertheless, as they drew closer Krancke ordered an alert for torpedo tracks.

The *Scheer's* ensign was run up. Her morse lamp flickered: 'Stop at once.' An officer on the bridge of the battleship wanted to know whether he should order a prize crew. 'No time,' said Krancke. 'We must sink her.'

Now came Krancke's most puzzling decision. After ordering the *Mopan* not to transmit, he told the crew of the freighter to take to the boats and pull towards the *Scheer*!

With the convoy just over the horizon the *Scheer* sat motionless, waiting for three boatloads of British sailors to row stolidly across the intervening sea, so that they might be taken on board as prisoners.

Before the *Mopan's* crew were taken on board, and as soon as he had a clear shot, Krancke ordered the shelling of the freighter, using his 105mm anti-aircraft guns to punch a precise row of holes in her waterline.

It was 1605 hours before the battleship set off at full speed to intercept the convoy. Krancke had used up a precious hour in dealing with one medium-sized merchantman.

As the *Scheer* raced towards the forest of masts that were just appearing over the horizon all sixty-eight of the *Mopan*'s crew were being bundled into the signallers' quarters of the pocket battleship. One of them was sixteen-year-old Jimmy McIntosh from Belfast, the second radio officer.

When the enemy warship had first been identified Jimmy had tumbled eagerly up on deck, expecting to see his chief frantically signalling details of the sighting to base, Instead the youngster was told by the chief radio officer that no signal would be transmitted.

Naturally the *Mopan*'s crew knew about the convoy, having passed it only a few hours earlier. In the bowels of the German warship they argued back and forth about their failure to warn the unsuspecting ships.

'But if we had signalled,' someone said, 'the *Jervis Bay* would only have tried to rescue us. She would have been destroyed.'

What is certain is that the crew of the *Mopan* would never have been allowed to take to their boats if a warning message had been attempted. They owed their lives to the decision of their captain not to send a signal. In addition, of course, Krancke had delayed the inevitable attack on the convoy by many valuable minutes when he decided to pick up the *Mopan*'s crew.

The role played by the *Mopan* in the *Jervis Bay* drama goes down in history as a harmless one. By delaying

Krancke as the crew of the banana boat did, they did more to save the lives of the seamen in Convoy HX 84 than anything else that could have happened. But the *Mopan*'s captain could not have known this at the time.

As for Krancke, he had now made it certain that a majority of the ships in the convoy would escape in the darkness once the action began. The *Scheer* could only hope now to make perhaps one pass at the merchantmen whilst they were in close formation, and then to mop perhaps two or three more ships up on the return course, before darkness made further sightings out of the question.

The *Mopan*'s sinking did, in fact, serve to alert the convoy to some extent. A lookout on the *Rangitiki* saw smoke to the north at 1545 hours, and Captain Barnett informed Admiral Maltby, commodore of the convoy, on board the *Cornish City*, and Captain Fegen on the *Jervis Bay*. At once Fegen brought his officers to the alert and directed that a special watch be kept on the horizon to the north.

At this time no general message was passed to the ships in the convoy, although a certain air of urgency was felt by those in the vicinity of the escort and the *Cornish City* because of the flag signals that were passing.

Certainly there was no alarm on board the *Kenbane Head*. Captain Milner was below in his cabin. Up on the bridge French, the mate, was keeping an eye on the *Anna Bulgari* ahead and the *Varoy* to port. Station-keeping was easier than usual on this trip. The *Kenbane Head* had no ships to starboard or astern.

Jimmy Dickey, the chief steward, was thinking of starting the routine for the evening meal. Billy McBride and the other sailors on the twelve to four watch were looking forward to seeing their reliefs soon, and Hugh McCready, the only passenger, was sitting in his cabin, feeling bored, and wondering what things were like at home.

Donald McKay, one of the ABs, was feeling a bit low. He seemed to be depressed in general these days. Donald, from Middletown in County Armagh, had served nearly four years of his deck apprenticeship in the Head Line, then suddenly he had tired of working for the few shillings a month that the terms of the apprenticeship demanded. He surrendered his indenture contract and signed on as an AB at £9.10 a month. He could still become an officer, but he had added three or four years to his timetable. This could have been on his mind, adding to his general low spirits, occasioned, understandably enough, by the mounting casualties among his comrades.

He had written to his sister Grace from Montreal, 'I am sure you wondered did I ever get across the treacherous ocean. Isn't this damn war terrible? I don't know what to make of it. I only hope that you … are spared the horrors of it.

'The poor sailor's job is the worst at present. Us poor fellows never know if we shall ever reach home again once we go to sea. The other day a big Elder Dempster boat was torpedoed off the north of Ireland and nineteen lost, but, Grace, sailors don't care. We don't be afraid until we get the bang.'

It was just about 1635 hours when the lookouts on the *Jervis Bay*, scanning the area to the north where the smoke had been reported, saw an unidentified ship. By 1645 hours she could be distinguished as a warship. The superstructure seemed to mark her out as a battleship. Someone hazarded a guess that it was the *Rodney*. At 1655 hours Captain Fegen sounded 'action stations'. Down on the deck a gunner's mate was guessing that the stranger was the *Ramilles*; a nearby gunner argued that it was the *Resolution*, and a range-taker reckoned it was the *Barham*.

Fegen ordered the Chief Yeoman of Signals to make the challenge. The *Jervis Bay* began to race ahead of the convoy. Her morse lamp flashed 'A ... A ... A'.

That's not an ordinary morse lamp,' said Krancke on the *Scheer*. 'It's too powerful. That's a warship.'

The *Jervis Bay* was well ahead of the convoy now. Behind her the sea was filled with ships, right across the southern horizon. When she was ten miles off the *Scheer* the escort sent up red rockets. She and other ships near her began to make smoke.

The *Scheer* turned to port to bring her broadside to bear. The 11-inch guns were to range on the auxiliary cruiser and the medium guns were to open up on a nearby tanker. The *Jervis Bay* turned to port. Krancke saw this as a manoeuvre to protect the *Rangitiki*, floating high in the water behind the AMC.

The *Castilian* was making signals for the benefit of the ships at the rear of the convoy. French, on the bridge of the *Kenbane Head*, called Milner from his cabin to take command.

The commodore signalled the convoy: 'Emergency turn forty degrees starboard.'

As the *Jervis Bay* closed with the *Scheer* Fegen ordered a signal hoisted: 'Prepare to scatter.'

At eight miles' range the *Scheer's* main armament opened up in an orange and black ripple along the ship's side. On the *Jervis Bay* the old hands said a prayer. They knew something of German gunnery.

A signal was tapped out by the *Jervis Bay* to the Admiralty: 'Enemy battleship 5245 N 3213 W.'

The first salvo was fifty yards short. The *Jervis Bay's* guns roared in reply. From the *Scheer's* bridge the AMC's flashes looked feeble.

On board the *Kenbane Head* someone shouted down the fo'c's'le steps: 'Come on up till ye see this!' and the whole of the watch below tumbled up on deck.

Captain Milner could see the exchanges of fire now. He considered using the *Kenbane Head's* gun, but there was a danger of hitting other ships in the convoy. The *Kenbane Head* began to lay smoke, as the other ships were doing. Milner put her on to a course of 255 degrees – a complete about-turn. On his starboard quarter the *Jervis Bay* was beginning to burn ...

Fogarty Fegen and his crew were now in the classical situation so dear to the hearts of the British – on the receiving end in a naval slaughtering match. The *Jervis Bay* was outgunned and outranged. The carnage on board the big liner was dreadful. The *Scheer's* 11-inch guns were doing massive damage to the fabric of the ship, and casualties among the crew had rendered the proper handling of the liner impossible.

The extensive woodwork throughout the *Jervis Bay* was well ablaze. A whole gun, its mounting and its entire crew were blown to pieces with one shell burst. The ship's steelwork was mangled and twisted and the deck was red hot. Great holes were torn in the hull again and again. Watertight doors buckled and jammed and living men were trapped below, their screams unheeded in the nightmarish din. The open deck was littered with dead men and parts of men.

Fogarty Fegen himself, after having had one arm blown off, was killed outright shortly before the *Jervis Bay* stopped and began slowly to sink.

The armed merchant cruiser had managed to attract the main armament of the *Scheer* for over twenty minutes. For part of that time the battleship had engaged and even damaged other ships in the convoy with her secondary armament, but eventually the heavy, medium and light guns were all turned on to the *Jervis Bay*.

Because Krancke could see one gun still firing on Fegen's ship.

And the darkness was now falling fast.

And the ships of Convoy HX 84 were making their escape in all directions.

Krancke was so concerned to avoid even slight damage to the *Scheer* that he concentrated the whole of his fire on a vessel that ought properly to have been left alone after half a dozen strikes with the main armament.

When Krancke's excessive caution regarding all-night shadowing followed by a dawn attack the next morning is taken into account it is not difficult to conclude that Fegen was faced by an excessively timid foe; one who was the opposite of swashbuckling. A captain who could not forget the example of Captain Langsdorff and the *Graf Spee*.

Add to this the incredible delay caused by the sinking of the *Mopan* and strong justification can be made for the claim that Krancke was also stupid on the day.

History shows that 32 of the 37 ships in Convoy HX 84

were saved by Fogarty Fegen and his men. The British will never let go of the belief that 32 ships' crews owed their safety to the fact that Fegen and 189 of his men laid down their lives for them.

Judging purely on the facts it would seem to be nearer the truth to say that Convoy HX 84 was saved by the timidity and the stupidity of Kapitan Theodor Krancke, one-time commanding officer of the German Naval Academy.

It would not even seem to be stretching belief too far to say that almost any other capital-ship commander in the German Navy, in the circumstances, would have polished off the *Jervis Bay* and at least a third of the convoy without even considering that the feat had been difficult.

The final proof of the botching of the attack by Krancke lies in the fact that the *Scheer* was somewhat lucky even in sinking five ships of the convoy besides the *Jervis Bay*.

In at least one, and possibly two cases, the pocket battleship only sank its victims because it had almost bumped into them in the darkness.

20

THE SLAUGHTER II
THE SINKING OF
THE *KENBANE HEAD*

No matter how badly Captain Theodor Krancke had handled the convoy attack there had to be victims among the merchantmen. There were too many slow-moving ships for things to be otherwise.

The *Scheer* had turned her medium guns on to a tanker when her main armament had first engaged the *Jervis Bay*. This ship was the *San Demetrio*. Krancke's shells had set her burning, but she had disappeared from the eyes of those on the *Scheer's* bridge, into the smokescreen laid down by the ships in the leading line.

Later, after it had turned away from the *Jervis Bay*, the battleship came upon the *San Demetrio* again. Fires were burning amidships but the ship was still making slow headway. As far as the Germans could see in the shadowy gloom, the tanker was unmanned, but the *Scheer* opened up nevertheless with several rounds from the medium guns.

Krancke now had his eye on the ship which he had placed second in importance to the *Jervis Bay*. This was the *Rangitiki*, sister-ship to the AMC *Rawalpindi*, sunk by the

Scharnhorst and *Gneisenau*, and to the *Rangitani*, sunk by the two German auxiliary cruisers *Komet* and *Orion*. Her wireless calls had identified her to the *Scheer*. Krancke believed her to be a troopship.

Captain Barnett of the *Rangitiki* made constant changes of course and speed to bluff the German gunners, but even so the *Scheer's* first two salvos landed only a few hundred yards off and the third one straddled her, with the nearest shell bursting only fifty yards away. Krancke's gunners believed that they had hit the *Rangitiki* by the time she disappeared into the smoke, but the only damage to the cargo liner was caused by shell fragments.

As it became clear that the *Scheer* had lost the *Rangitiki* Captain Barnett considered the immediate action to be taken regarding an escape route. It was necessary to make a judgement as to the raider's general intentions. Barnett quickly came to the conclusion that the battleship would not return north: that the attack on the convoy was not a one-off operation; that a protracted operation lay ahead of the raider, probably in the South Atlantic; and that the most likely direction the battleship would take right then to avoid naval pursuit was to the west.

Accordingly Barnett put his ship on to a north-westerly course in the darkness. He had guessed the enemy's intention exactly and saved his ship, crew and passengers in doing so.

From his bridge the captain of the *Rangitiki* could see that slower ships to the south and south-east were coming under attack. Two of them had been hit and were burning.

In fact, the *Scheer* had attacked the *Andalusian*, but she escaped undamaged. Then the battleship's guns were turned on the *Maidan*, sailing on a southerly course. She loomed up just to starboard of the raider and Krancke concentrated all his armament on her.

The *Maidan*, weighing 7,908 tons, had loaded iron, steel, brass, timber, tobacco and trucks at Baltimore before joining the convoy at Halifax. The trajectories of the tracer shells clearly showed in the darkness that every gun was scoring hits. Almost instantaneously with the opening of the attack fires raged on board the *Maidan* and sparks shot into the night sky.

Then the stricken ship began to heel over, slowly at first, then faster and faster. From stem to stern the merchantman was an intense ball of fire. So brightly was she burning that the watchers on the *Scheer* could see every detail of the scene. Suddenly the *Maidan* sank. There was a great, screaming hiss, as the flames met the sea. The blinding light went out for good. All hands were lost.

The other victim which the officers of the *Rangitiki* had seen burning was the *Trewellard*, a vessel of 5,200 tons. She had loaded in Boston a cargo of steel and pig iron. She, too, got the *Scheer's* full armament. The blaze was not so fierce, but the *Trewellard* went down in minutes; twenty-five of her crew managed to escape.

The *Scheer* had by then sunk two merchant ships and caused a third to be abandoned. Krancke was under the impression that he had caused far more damage than this. He had actually fired on the *San Demetrio* twice, believing – understandably in the circumstances – that it was two different ships and that each had been sunk. His chief gunnery officer, Commander Schumann, felt sure that he had scored vital hits on the *Rangitiki* before and after she had disappeared into the smoke.

Despite Krancke's apparent success, however, there were plenty of other fat merchantmen wallowing in the area. He put paid to one in a matter of minutes and left it blazing, then the *Scheer*'s radar apparatus located another target to the south-east. This was the *Beaverford*, ten thousand tons, bound for Liverpool from Montreal with foodstuffs, timber and munitions. The *Scheer* opened up with her 11-inch guns and scored three hits. Those in charge of the medium guns counted sixteen hits scored on the freighter.

She sank until her decks were awash. The deck cargo was keeping her afloat. Krancke ordered the crippled ship to be torpedoed.

When the torpedo struck the fore part of the *Beaverford*, she was lifted clean out of the water, then she heeled over and quickly sank.

When the *Scheer* had first opened fire on the *Beaverford* her wireless operator had sent out his last message: 'It's our turn now. So long. The master and crew of the *Beaverford*.'

All hands were lost.

The *Scheer*'s final victim was the *Fresno City*. By bad luck the five-thousand-ton sister to the *Cornish City* was on a westerly course. So was the *Scheer*. At 2155 hours, when the crew of the *Fresno City* had every reason to congratulate themselves on their escape, the *Scheer*'s lookouts called out urgently. There was an unexpected target only three thousand yards ahead. Using her searchlight for illumination, the pocket battleship sank the *Fresno City*, but twenty-five men got away in one of her boats and nine in another, including the master, Captain Lawson.

The battleship *Scheer* then made her escape, first to the west, then due south. Krancke had taken the lives of 190 naval officers and ratings, and 206 men of the merchant navy. He wirelessed home a claim that he had sunk 86,000 tons of shipping. In fact, he had sunk 47,495 tons – the *Jervis Bay*, *Maidan*, *Trewellard*, *Beaverford*, *Fresno City*.

In between sinking the *Trewellard* and the *Beaverford* one other ship was sunk – the *Kenbane Head*.

She was steering 255 degrees at the time. Captain Milner hadn't figured out the *Scheer*'s intentions. Captain Barnett of the *Rangitiki* had, and so too for that matter had Admiral Maltby, the commodore of the convoy, on board the *Cornish City* – Barnett and he shouted congratulations to each other later from ship to ship – but most of the ships' masters in the convoy just turned their vessels away from the *Scheer* and left it at that, hoping for the best.

The scene on board the Head Line ship was one to strike fear into the heart of any seaman.

Over to the north the battered hulk of the *Jervis Bay* was still blazing. Several miles nearer the burning tanker *San Demetrio* could be seen. The taut figures on the bridge of the *Kenbane Head* had seen the whole horizon to their starboard quarter explode in one massive eruption as the *Maidan* blew up.

Looking aft over their boiling wake Milner and French, Leckey and Bell and the apprentice Crangle had winced involuntarily as the *Trewellard* received her death-blow. And always, throughout the headlong flight since the *Scheer* had first appeared, a menacing shadow on the northern skyline, there was the ripple of the warship's guns, and the sound of the shell-bursts.

They still thought they would make it. The darkness ahead was comforting. The night sea and sky to the west, beyond the stem of the *Kenbane Head*, promised safety. It seemed to the watchers on the bridge that their ship was leaving that part of the ocean where the night was being torn by jagged orange flame: that they were on the brink of escape. It was 1815 hours.

Suddenly a star shell burst overhead, bathing the freighter in cruel, blue-white light. The *Kenbane Head* was outlined against the night backdrop. It was as though, in that unearthly illumination, she was the only ship in the sea and that the ocean itself had frozen.

The tired little ship seemed to pause, immobile for an instant of time, turning her throat to receive the death-blow from the powerful, invisible enemy poised outside in the darkness.

Krancke was worried because he thought a gun was firing from the *Kenbane Head*'s poop deck at the *Scheer*. This was not so. His fear was groundless. He let the 5,225-ton freighter, with its pitifully thin plating, have a salvo from the main armament in the course of other bombardments. Then the *Scheer* raced on to intercept the next target, leaving the *Kenbane Head* listing and in flames.

When the firing first started, Milner had ordered the confidential papers to be placed in a weighted bag and thrown overboard. Then the shells landed and the *Kenbane Head* began to disintegrate. The first salvo put the steering gear out of action, set fire to the poop hatch and magazine and carried away the main and emergency aerials. Further hits blew gaping holes in the hull, striking the vessel in Nos 1 and 4 holds. Then she was hit repeatedly in the engine room. The funnel casing was smashed and the gun was blown away. The starboard lifeboat was reduced to matchwood.

Milner had mustered all hands at the bridge deck to board No. 2 lifeboat when the final salvo burst, causing casualties among the crew. The port lifeboat was lowered only to fill on reaching the water.

The wind was south-east, Force 4, with a slight sea and moderate swell. The ship was tossing sufficiently to make the job of climbing back on board her extremely difficult. Those who were fit managed it, but many were left in the sinking lifeboat, wounded, or floating in the sea around the ship, where they had fallen after trying in vain to climb on to the burning *Kenbane Head*.

Paddy Cahill, the radio officer, had already sent a distress call.

At this stage a plaintive voice was heard from the crow's nest, asking whether he might come down. The lookout had been overlooked!

Dickey and Blair, McBride plus the two apprentices, Gerry Crangle and Norman Walsh, all managed to get back on board, as did Captain Milner and many others. Gerry Crangle went down to his cabin for − of all things − a picture of a girlfriend. Jimmy Dickey managed to get into his room and collect an overcoat. Bill McBride nipped down into the fo'c's'le and got a cork life jacket for the apprentice, Walsh.

Those on board the *Kenbane Head* managed to slide a raft over the side. Then they discovered that the jolly boats had miraculously escaped the barrage. These small, open boats, without flotation tanks or stores, used mainly for recreational purposes, were lowered under the direction of the master, and the second mate, George Leckey. The boats were lashed to the raft, the survivors distributed themselves between the three and they rowed – four oars to a boat – away from the *Kenbane Head*.

Many of the survivors, especially engine room and galley staff, were very lightly clad to face the rigours of an open boat. One or two were already dead in the water. As the boats moved slowly away from the ship, past the partly sunken lifeboat, Crangle saw two engine room staff dead inside. They were dressed only in singlet and trousers. The *Kenbane Head*, although listing badly and burning, did not sink until 1930 hours; her end was watched by the survivors from a few hundred yards away.

As the night wore on the wind got up to Force 7 with a heavy swell. Captain Milner was on the raft, the mate, French, was in charge of one boat and Leckey, the second mate, was in charge of the other boat. All told there were thirty-seven men still surviving out of forty-four.

That night of 5–6 November was cruelly cold. Soon a number of the men were already in severe shock and had lost consciousness. At around 0300 hours the burning *San Demetrio* drifted down on them. There was no one on board. A member of the *Kenbane Head*'s crew wanted them all to board the tanker, but they were overruled by the master.

They were in real danger from their proximity to the tanker. The huge bows, now towering over the raft and jolly boats, looked like catching the painter and pushing them under. Captain Milner ordered the jolly boat commanded by Leckey to cast off from the other two and make its way around the other side of the *San Demetrio*. As the little boat parted from them Milner told Leckey to keep in touch by morse lamp.

Flashes were seen in the distance a short time later, but by the time the other boat and raft had negotiated the length of the *San Demetrio*, Leckey's jolly boat had disappeared. This boat, with its nine occupants, was never seen again. Only twenty-eight were now left.

Somehow a majority of the men in the remaining boat and raft managed to stay active in the bitter cold. They worked hard on the little boat to keep its head to the sea, and this kept them occupied, but on the raft all they could do was exercise feebly and listen to Milner's occasional words of encouragement.

Next morning they found that eight of their number were dead, four on the raft and four in the boat. Crangle and one of the sailors put the bodies from the boat overboard. There was no ceremony: just a whispered 'Rest in Peace' by the eighteen-year-old apprentice.

This left room on the boat; those on the raft transferred over, cutting the raft adrift. There were now twenty survivors to face a long, weary day. The waves were ten to fifteen feet and it was vital that the boat's head be kept to the sea. The first ration of water was passed around on the afternoon of 6 November.

A lone seabird – a fulmar – swooped near them and they talked of catching it, but it was only talk. The bird gave them no chance.

A long, long night lay ahead. The weather had abated a

little and the sky had cleared. The bright planets were mistaken for the lights of ships. Some thought they saw rockets in the distant sky. Somehow they made it to dawn on 7 November.

The survivors were now almost spent. Each one sat, huddled and shivering, moving only when the turn to man an oar came around. By early afternoon on 7 November all hope had gone.

Suddenly a ship was sighted heading roughly in their direction from the east. They tried to row with all speed towards it. She passed only a cable's distance from the tiny boat. To their dismay her answering pennant was at the dip. She had not seen them. Those who had Acme distress whistles blew them ferociously.

Then, to their relief and wild excitement, the answering pennant shot up to the top triatic stay. They had been sighted! Willing hands pulled them up the ladder; tots of comforting rum were poured into empty stomachs.

The ship was the *Gloucester City*. Her master, on learning of the action from his radio operator, had courageously slowed his westward progress and directed his ship to look for survivors. He picked up seven boatloads in all – ninety-two men. There were twenty-five from the *Trewellard*, twenty-four from the *Fresno City*, twenty-three from the *San Demetrio* – which was eventually re-boarded and sailed back home by the rest of her crew – and twenty from the *Kenbane Head*.

It was 13 November before the *Gloucester City* docked in St John's, Newfoundland. It was only then that the families of living and dead alike from the *Kenbane Head*'s crew learned the fate of their loved ones. They had been alerted only a few days earlier to the possibility of calamitous news.

The tiny village of Ballyhalbert on the County Down coast was a place of prayers and tears and sleeplessness for those few days. Four of the *Kenbane Head*'s deck crew, Boyd, Miller, Fullerton and Pritchard came from there.

The little post office stayed open late on 14 November to receive the telephone call that the company had promised. The information came, cruelly, in two calls. After a delay the news came through that Pritchard had not survived: Boyd, Miller and Fullerton had.

In nearby Ballywalter the wife of Belshaw, the ship's carpenter, was told that her husband would not be returning.

The messages were going out all over Ulster. The *Kenbane Head* was lost. Many men were missing.

Meanwhile, in St John's, Newfoundland, the master of the *Kenbane Head* was writing his report. It was a short, abrupt one, in keeping with his temperament. The shelling and sinking, the deaths and agony and suffering of forty-five hours duration was compressed into two foolscap pages of typing.

A third page in Milner's report called the final roll. Here it is:

Survived. Total 20 men.
T.F. Milner, Master; W. French, Chief Officer; W. Bell, 3rd Officer; G. Crangle, Apprentice; N. Walsh, Apprentice; J. McQuillan, S. Boyd, F. Miller, W. McBride and D. Fullerton, deck crew; W.J. McIlroy, Chief Engineer; T. Smith, 3rd Engineer; A. McDonald, Greaser; J. Swain, J. McMichael and J. Barry, firemen; J. Dickey, Chief Steward;

F. McCaw, 2nd Steward; R. Drinkwater, Gunner; and
H. McCready, passenger.

No 3 boat missing. Total 9 men.
G. Leckey, 2nd Officer; H. Carson, 2nd Engineer; P. Cahill,
1st Radio Officer; J. Belshaw, carpenter; W. Wright,
Boatswain; D. Donovan, lamptrimmer; D. McKay, AB;
B. Henry, fireman; and H. Bloor, assistant cook.

Died and buried from No. 4 boat and raft. Total 8 men.
L. Graves, 2nd Radio Officer; J. Laidlaw, storekeeper;
J. McGuigan, donkeyman; R.J. Moore, 2nd cook;
G. Heatley, chief cook; J.L. McGuigan, H. Shaw and
D. Davies, firemen.

Missing and dead after No. 2 lifeboat filled. 7 men.
D. Wilson, 4th Engineer; R. Green, Apprentice;
D. Allister and D. Pritchard, deck crew; R. Primmer,
assistant steward; J. Emerson, fireman ...

And M. McAughtry, fireman

He was killed right at the start.

Billy McBride saw him trying to climb up to the *Kenbane Head*'s deck after the lifeboat filled. He must have been wounded. He fell back into the lifeboat. Beside Jim Emerson.

Mart was one of the engine room staff that Gerry Crangle saw dead in the lifeboat when the jolly boats were moving away from the ship's side.

That's how my brother was lost.

The *Kenbane Head*'s position when she was sunk was 5226 N 3234 W. Just twenty miles south-west of the spot where the *Jervis Bay* lies.

21

THE AFTERMATH

Strangely enough I do remember the radio announce-
ment about the *Jervis Bay* convoy. I rarely paid attention
to the news, but I remember that. Probably it was because
a convoy of merchant ships was involved.

I remember sprawling across a bed in a barrack room and
listening to a lively discussion on the subject. One chap was
saying he was glad he wasn't in the Navy. 'Christ,' he said,
'imagine finding yourself on a ship like the *Jervis Bay*.You'd
have no bloody chance!'

'Well then,' I couldn't help intervening, 'how would you
like to work on a merchant ship? They've got even less
chance.' Even then I couldn't understand why the English
always looked for bravery in the Royal Navy and
completely ignored the crews of the ships which the Navy
were signally failing to protect. I got into a heated
argument with a guy whose brother sailed in destroyers and
blinded him with science.

It was on Tuesday 19 November that Jack's letter came. I
was working late and was sleeping in camp. I got back to
my barrack room at ten o'clock at night, absolutely
whacked.The letter was on my bed. It had been addressed
by Jack, which was nothing unusual. He often addressed

Mother's letters to me. She wrote to me once a week regularly and I had grown accustomed to the content of her letter. Mrs so-and-so had met her in the butcher's and was asking for me. Tommy's regiment was thinking of moving to England. Jim was in the Auxiliary Fire Service now. Wasn't this war awful? I let the letter lie unopened.

I lay on the bed, unwinding. Jock Haran was sprawled on the bed beside me. A Welshman called Ginger Crowe was on the one opposite. We had returned from the hangars together.

'Coming over for supper Paddy?' Jock Haran was sitting up, knife, fork and mug in hand

'Right,' I said, wearily.

'Hang on chaps.' Ginger Crowe was always trying to trail after Jock Haran, Jake Thomson and myself. Everywhere we went he tended to turn up.

'I'll not be a minute,' he said. I saw that he was reading a letter. This reminded me … I picked up mine.

'I don't know how I am going to tell you this,' Jack wrote. 'You and Marriott were so close. His ship was in that convoy in the Atlantic that was attacked by the German raider. He is missing, believed dead ...'

I stood up. The room seemed to sway. My breath caught. I began to choke. Pushing someone's hand aside I dropped the letter and ran out into the darkness. I tried to push my knuckles into my mouth. Then I found myself on the ground, kneeling, drumming clenched fists on my thighs.

I wasn't crying. It was a sort of steady, thin scream.

Someone was holding me. Jock Haran. Paddy, Paddy, there there Paddy. What is it? Come on Paddy.

Down at the perimeter track. Still with Jock. A long way

from the billet. Mart Mart Mart. No. No. No.

We walked right round the perimeter track. All the way. Jock Haran told me how he had cried when he lost his mother. Every time I tried to talk I choked up.

I don't remember how that night went in. There wasn't any more crying. Just stunned disbelief. Mart Mart Mart Mart …

Next morning an interview with the station warrant officer. The lads at the hangar had a whip-round and handed me a couple of quid, sheepishly. The train and the boat, and home to a week of forced cheerfulness in front of Mother. You never know. He might be a prisoner. Never mind what the company says.

Back in camp again I thought about things for a couple of weeks. Then I asked the engineering officer could I see him please. Personal matter.

'Well. What is it?' Impatiently. He was a flight lieutenant. Well-built. Dark. Incisive type.

'I want to go for aircrew, sir.'

'What!' He was genuinely astonished. 'Aircrew? You?' I said nothing. I had polished my buttons and boots as they had never before been polished. I was a picture. Gleaming. Stiff as a ramrod.

'Your request is denied. Anything else?'

'No sir.' I saluted, went back to work.

The long working days continued. I stuck them out without getting into any sort of trouble. Kept my temper in check. Grafted away with the rest.

I began to learn the morse code. The Airspeed Oxford had a downward flashing light; I coaxed one of the wireless fitters to make simple signals on the lamp for me to take down. I noticed Tommy Roe, the engineering officer, watching me at this once, but he didn't object.

In March 1941 I stood before his desk at attention again. 'I want to go for aircrew, please sir,' I said.

'Look,' he said. 'With your record I can't afford to recommend you. Flying is a highly disciplined business. I couldn't possibly wish you on any crew.' He looked at me speculatively. 'What would you like to train for?' he asked.

'Navigator,' I told him.

'That's a tough course,' he said. He stared at me for another moment. Then he shook his head. 'Sorry, Paddy,' he said.

That use of Paddy was a good sign. I went back to work, praying that he would be spared to stay on the station for as long as I needed him.

In the middle of 1941 they made me an aircraftman first class. In the autumn I became a leading aircraftman rigger. I had come to a dead stop with my flying studies. I needed the classroom now.

November 1941. In front of Tommy Roe.

'I want to go for aircrew, please sir.'

'Why?' A breakthrough. A palpable breakthrough!

'I believe I can make a better contribution as a navigator, sir.'

'What are your educational qualifications?'

'None, sir.'

'What are your maths like?'

'Quite good, sir.'

The next question, when it came, nearly made me cheer.

'What do you know for example about logarithms?'

I drew a deep breath. 'The log of a number,' I said

exultantly, 'is the number of powers to which ten must be raised in order to equal that number. One hundred equals ten to the power of two: the log of a hundred is two.'

(And though we haven't met for months may the Lord protect and keep you, Martha, I said, now and forever more.)

'I don't know whether you'll ever make it through your course,' said Tommy Roe, 'but you're welcome to try as far as I'm concerned.' He stood up. 'What sort of aircraft do you want to fly in?' he asked.

'The sort that sink ships,' I told him.

I had never bargained for anything like the extent of training that I had to undergo. Shipping-strike aircraft had two-man crews, so the navigator had to be a jack of all trades. I was trained in England as a radio operator first, then went to Ontario, Canada, to train as a navigator. After that I went to Prince Edward Island for ocean navigation training and ship recognition.

Back in England we had to learn to act as radio operator on Avro Ansons for one half of a training trip and navigate the aircraft during the other half. We picked up Bristol Beaufighters and test-flew them out over the Atlantic from a base on Islay. Then we flew out from Cornwall to North Africa in time for the ending of the war there, but there was still more training awaiting us. Near Suez we did a course on dropping torpedoes and finally wound up learning how to fire sixty-pound rockets.

By the time I finally reached an operational squadron at the end of 1943 the Germans had no naval forces of any significance left in the Adriatic or the Mediterranean. By August 1944 I had flown twenty operational sorties – convoy strikes, harbour strikes and night intruding operations over enemy airfields. So far I had attacked only light shipping dependent more on air cover than on sizeable naval escorts.

But on 31 August 1944 in the Aegean Sea I was navigator of the aircraft leading two flights each of three Beaufighters. We carried eight rockets under our wings. We were armed with four Hispano 20mm cannon and six machine guns. We were flying the most formidable shipping-strike aircraft in the world. I even had a Browning .303 machine gun to myself in the rear cockpit.

Suddenly someone called. A sighting. A destroyer, with an armed merchantman. Somebody else identified them. Both German. Johnny Bates, my pilot, led the six aircraft in a circuit around the targets.

'The warship. It's ours,' he said. He carried out an air briefing. First three aircraft were to go in as anti-flak and strike on the warship; second three simultaneously to take the merchantman.

The flak was coming now. 80mm, 40mm, and 20mm – the last was the worst. It was everywhere.

My head was under the rubber hood of the ASV radar: '3,500 yards,' I called. '3,200 … Hey, Johnny.'

'Yes, Paddy?' The pilot sounded urgent. He thought I was going to give a fighter warning. There were bound to be ME 109s about.

'When you hit that ship,' I said, 'really hurt the bastard.'

'Will do,' he said.

'1,500 … 1,300 … FIRE!' I yelled, and eight beautiful,

gorgeous sixty-pound high explosive rockets went howling down like banshees towards the grey, lean target below.

In the midst of the whooshing flak, in a sky peppered with crimson and grey and black smudges, our Beaufighter arrowed on to the target, cannons yammering and filling the inside of the aircraft with eye-watering, acrid, cordite fumes. We pulled out of the dive at one hundred feet, and I opened up with my solitary Browning, spraying the smoking deck hopefully. Then we dropped to sea level, and I gave my pilot a snap course for base. Behind us we left two mushrooms of smoke and orange flame.

I relaxed, looking out of the open rear window; lit up a forbidden cigarette.

'Well, Johnny,' I said, 'we didn't exactly get ourselves a pocket battleship, but at least we introduced ourselves to the German Navy at long last.'

'What the hell are you going on about?' my pilot wanted to know.

'Oh, never mind,' I said. 'It's a long story.'

22

THE FINAL CURTAIN

They gave Captain Edward Stephen Fogarty Fegen the Victoria Cross. Posthumously, of course. The award was made with remarkably little delay.

'For valour in challenging hopeless odds and giving his life to save the many ships it was his duty to protect,' the citation ran.

The battleship *Scheer* sailed southwards after the *Jervis Bay* action. It was possible that the redoubtable Force H might have intercepted her on the way, but Admiral Somerville needed this formidable battle formation for another operation in the Mediterranean.

The *Scheer* had left behind a state of panic and confusion that exceeded even Hitler's expectations. The sudden appearance of a pocket battleship in the North Atlantic had caused serious alarm in Whitehall.

Convoys which had already set course were recalled. The Canadian ports were hopelessly congested. It was not until 17 November that convoys began to sail for Britain from Halifax again.

Escorts were greatly strengthened. Destroyers and even

cruisers were taken off other duties and put to convoy escort work. As far as the Allied war effort was concerned the effect was far more serious than the actual losses in lives, cargo-space and materials had been.

In April 1941 the armed merchant cruiser *Voltaire* was sunk by the German auxiliary cruiser *Thor*. Captain Blackburn, in command of the *Voltaire*, had sailed the HX convoy routes as second in command to Fegen. With the loss of the *Voltaire* and ninety of her crew the British Admiralty decided finally to take the armed merchant cruisers off convoy escort work.

Captain Theodor Krancke continued to take scalps on his southward voyage. On 24 November he sank the *Port Hobart* south-east of Bermuda. The Admiralty believed this to be the work of an auxiliary cruiser.

On 1 December the *Scheer* sank the *Tribesman*. Soon the supply ship *Nordmark* was crammed with British merchant marine crews, including those of the *Mopan, Tribesman, Port Hobart* and the *Duquesa*. The last-named, a refrigerated vessel carrying foodstuffs, was towed behind the *Scheer* for some time as a sort of floating goodies-basket. The *Scheer's* crew, suntanned and at the peak of their confidence, were fed like gladiators out of the *Duquesa's* holds.

The pocket battleship went on to sink sixteen ships in addition to the *Jervis Bay*. By the time she tied up in Kiel on 1 April 1941 before wildly-cheering crowds, she had steamed 46,419 sea miles, during which time she had not once sighted a real warship.

The *Scheer* had carried out exactly the function that she was built for. Every member of her crew was awarded the Iron Cross.

Theodor Krancke later became a shore-based admiral. He was naval representative at Hitler's HQ in East Prussia. His last significant role in history was a passive one. It was to Krancke that a furious Hitler, on New Year's Day 1943, gave the instruction that the heavy ships were to be paid off.

'They are a needless drain on men and materials!' Hitler yelled. This outburst followed an unsuccessful attack by the battleship *Lutzow* on an Allied convoy bound for Russia.

In fact the big ships were not paid off, although they remained tied up for some time. The *Scharnhorst* was in action on Christmas Day and Boxing Day 1943, attempting, in severe gale conditions, to intercept a convoy heading for Murmansk.

It was the *Scharnhorst's* last action. She was sunk by the battleship *Duke of York* and attendant cruisers and destroyers near the North Cape on 26 December.

Of her crew only 36 survived; 1,932 were lost, including Admiral Erich Bay.

The end of the *Admiral Scheer* was an ignominious one. In mid-1944 she and the other pocket battleship *Lutzow*, together with the heavy cruiser *Prince Eugen*, were used as extra artillery off the Baltic coast, helping the retreating rearguard of the German Army.

Their powerful guns checked the Russian advance wherever they were deployed, but finally the ships had to be withdrawn due to lack of ammunition and fuel. Their gun barrels were worn smooth.

The cruiser *Hipper* was destroyed by aerial bombing on 2 April 1945, whilst in Kiel. On 9 April, in the same port, the once-proud battleship *Admiral Scheer* was hit repeatedly by British bombers and capsized, a total loss.

So, really, the British Navy never did get her.

As far as the Battle of the Atlantic is concerned, Germany began to lose after the first two years of the war. By that time Allied ship production was exceeding the tonnage being sunk and the Allied naval forces were equipped with superior radar equipment. When in 1943 escort carriers began to close the air gap in the mid–Atlantic the U–boats were finished, although many personal outstanding successes still lay ahead for the U–boat commanders.

A surprisingly little-known contributory reason for the U–boats' failure was the practice by them of transmitting frequent sighting reports. The British high-frequency direction-finding equipment was easily able to pinpoint the submarines and 'home' ships or aircraft on to them.

The accelerating pace of the U–boats' defeat is illustrated by the following details of their losses:

SEPTEMBER–DECEMBER	1939	9
	1940	22
	1941	35
	1942	76
	1943	237
	1944	241
JANUARY–MAY	1945	153

But by the time the Germans began to lose their grip on the war the British merchant service had already been severely mauled. Most of the thirty-two thousand merchant seamen lost in the war had already died by the time the Navy and the RAF began to play a significant attacking role in the Battle of the Atlantic in the middle of 1942.

And what of the Head Line crews? Most of the fleet had been lost by the end of 1941 and the crews who survived were dispersed throughout other merchant ships. Many of these Ulstermen were to be pleasantly surprised by the improved living conditions that they met, especially on the American-built ships. Not surprisingly, such men were never again prepared to work in ships where they were expected to carry their hot water across a pitching deck and down the steep fo'c's'le steps, after finishing a hard watch in the stokehold.

Some Head Line men survived earlier attacks only to die when the tide was turning their way. One of these was Jim Swain, a fireman, who had managed to survive the *Kenbane Head*'s sinking. Jim had a sweetheart in Carrickfergus, Mary O'Hara, who remembers vividly her relief on learning that he had safely arrived in Newfoundland.

He came home to recuperate, rested until the salt water blisters on his body had healed, and set off to sea again. Jim and Mary had meantime decided not to marry for a bit.

They took their time deciding on a wedding date. Mary bitterly recalls this today, for Jim Swain was lost in March 1943, with the rest of his shipmates, when the *Fort Lamy* was torpedoed. Her cargo was TNT.

Jimmy Dickey was torpedoed in the *Fanad Head*, shelled and cast adrift from the *Kenbane Head*, and torpedoed again in the *Dunaff Head*. By some miracle he saw the war through, and now he lives in peaceful retirement in Scotland.

Gerry Crangle and Norman Walsh, the two apprentices from the *Kenbane Head* are both ships' masters with plenty of sailing in them yet.

Billy McBride gave up the sea after the war. He doesn't miss it one bit.

Hugh McCready, the *Kenbane Head*'s passenger, never did join Britain's armed forces. Instead he went back to the States after recovering from his ordeal, and eventually saw active service in the US Air Force. He returned after the war to Northern Ireland. Tragically Hugh McCready died suddenly in 1970, leaving a widow and a son in his pleasant house on the shores of Strangford Lough.

In 1947, outward bound to Sydney NSW, an old ex-Head Line seadog came off watch on board the SS *Sneaton*, owned by Headlam and Son, Whitby. With only a couple of exceptions he had sailed in Head Line ships for forty-four years. His last trip in a ship of the Ulster Steamship Company had been in the *Dunaff Head* when she had been torpedoed in March 1941.

Before he had time for his tub the old-timer was told that the master wanted to see him. Somewhat nervously he presented himself at the captain's quarters.

He was astonished when the captain of the *Sneaton* greeted him with a hearty handshake, and a generous glass of whiskey.

'I've been keeping an eye on the date,' he told the mystified Belfast man.

'Do you happen to know that this is an anniversary?'

The grizzled seaman shook his head.

'Today, Mark,' the captain said, 'you are fifty years at sea.'

It could never have happened in the impersonal Head Line. Captain and donkeyman sat in the master's quarters for a couple of hours, yarning and 'bevying', as Mart McAughtry put it.

It was in the *Sneaton*, four years later, that my father, then sixty-nine years old, sailed on his final voyage. En route to Australia he was taken ill. The ship was diverted to Cuba, where he was put ashore for treatment. The captain of the *Sneaton* made generous provision for the old seaman's treatment, including his air fare home. It was not needed. My father is buried today in Santa Cruz del Sur in Cuba.

His grave is a long, long way from the resting-place of his sweetheart, in the shadow of the Black Mountain, in County Antrim.

And he would not have wished to rest so far away from the place where Mart died. But that was the chance that sailors took in those times.

'He was one of a vanishing breed,' my father's captain wrote. 'Seamen of his quality are as rare as gold dust.' We are proud of the tribute in our family.

Mart, too, is entitled to his special epitaph. But perhaps he won't mind sharing one used often by the Germans who killed him, and who died themselves, in turn: